The National Cherry Festival in Traverse City

The NATIONAL CHERRY FESTIVAL IN TRAVERSE CITY

Blessing of the Blossoms

BROOKS VANDERBUSH

Charleston · London
THE History PRESS

Published by The History Press
Charleston, SC 29403
www.historypress.net

Copyright © 2014 by Brooks Vanderbush
All rights reserved

Cover courtesy of the History Center of Traverse City.

First published 2014, Second printing 2014

Manufactured in the United States

ISBN 978.1.62619.426.7

Library of Congress CIP data applied for.

Notice: The information in this book is true and complete to the best of our knowledge. It is offered without guarantee on the part of the author or The History Press. The author and The History Press disclaim all liability in connection with the use of this book.

All rights reserved. No part of this book may be reproduced or transmitted in any form whatsoever without prior written permission from the publisher except in the case of brief quotations embodied in critical articles and reviews.

CONTENTS

Foreword, by Trevor Tkach   7
Acknowledgements   9
Introduction   11

1. From Log to Cherry   13
2. Cherry Explosion   23
3. The Festival Goes Nuclear   37
4. The President Arrives   47
5. Big Hair and the Arnolds   57
6. Our Modern Festival   65
7. The Queen in Her Own Words   79
8. The Town that Cherry Sells   89
9. The Stories   99
10. Get Thee to the Festival!   115

Index   117
About the Author   125

FOREWORD

It's easy to celebrate cherries because cherries are fun! And you can be sure that Traverse City is one of the most fun places in the world, as it produces 75 percent of the nation's tart cherry crop, making Traverse City the "Cherry Capital of the World" and, thus, home of the National Cherry Festival.

Back when the festival first began, we had just switched from a lumbering community to a farming economy. You really have to give a lot of credit to our forefathers as they had the insight to establish somewhat of a tourism-based economy in the area. They used the Cherry Festival as a way to promote that tourism. They also saw that there was an agricultural component to it as well, so the cherry was used as a unique fruit that they could talk about downstate and in the region to attract tourists and also to draw investors to open businesses and buy vacation properties and such. It was a good marriage of tourism and cherries.

The mission of the National Cherry Festival to this day is to celebrate and promote cherries and community involvement in the Grand Traverse region. The cherry is still very much the pinnacle thing at the festival. We are very fortunate in this region. We live in an area that is not only beautiful, and one in which people want to recreate, but also one of the few places in the world wherein we can grow the caliber and variety of cherries that we are able to grow. This is a story that we can tell that other resort towns can't. It's really a fun, unique thing. The cherry is extremely important in both our marketing and our programming. A lot of the work we do, to this day, is for our local farmers and this exciting crop.

Foreword

The cherry makes this area what it is. You couldn't have this sort of success with something like the Traverse City Festival. The cherry has really set it apart.

The celebration of Traverse City's signature fruit has drawn millions of visitors from across the globe seeking a unique, family friendly experience that revels in agricultural and cultural tradition. The National Cherry Festival preserves the traditions that we all cherish by offering generations of fun to all that attend.

This festival is a part of the culture. This isn't just someone's little brainchild festival; this is a part of the fabric of the community in Northern Michigan. It's Americana. It's been around long enough that it's been ingrained into our minds over the years for all of the right reasons and for so long that it has stuck.

I grew up here, and I have vivid memories of parades as a five year old. I've ridden on floats, and I was a prince. I went through it all. Then, there was getting older within the festival and going to my first big concert at the Cherry Festival. There are so many life memories attached to this one singular event that happens every summer in Traverse City. It's something that's larger than life. It's a festival for all people.

There are two thousand volunteers who are totally invested in this festival every year. We also have hundreds of businesses locally that donate time and money because they understand the economic impact and what the festival means to the culture and to the region.

The National Cherry Festival is bigger than just an event. This isn't just a festival. It's our way of life. It's who we are. The Cherry Festival will always be here. I could get hit by a bus tomorrow, and there will still be a Cherry Festival. You can't say that about a lot of things in this region. A lot of the time, whatever it is has a connection back to one person. Not so with this festival. I don't think anyone is going to let that go in this community because it is their festival. The community owns this festival, and the festival is there for and because of the community.

The National Cherry Festival is an American homecoming. It's the summertime dream of every child and every adult's memory of their favorite hometown festival. A venerated agricultural celebration, the Cherry Festival takes you back to a simpler time and place, where a queen and her court still reign and a parade through downtown is still the most popular event of the year.

—Trevor Tkach
National Cherry Festival executive director, 2014

ACKNOWLEDGEMENTS

Through the whirlwind that was the creation of this book, my little tornado has passed through the lives and the offices of so many. Each and every one of them helped me pull together the bits and pieces that make up this wonderful celebration's story.

Without them, this book would not exist. So allow me a moment to thank the folks who helped me the most in this venture.

Thank you to the lovely ladies of the History Center of Traverse City, who worked so hard to make my wacky schedule fit theirs and who were always there whenever a need arose. This book would not exist without the efforts and patience of Peg Siciliano, Maddie Buteyn and Laura Wilson. You guys rock!

Thank you also to the awesome people who inhabit the National Cherry Festival offices, especially Trevor Tkach, the festival's executive director, and Jessica Schlimme, the festival's volunteer manager.

Thank you to Lawrence and Lucille Wakefield, whom I never met but whose pictorial book on the festival was an outstanding resource into the 1980s. Thanks also to the *Ludington Daily News* for covering the festival so voraciously.

I also want to send a shout-out to the folks who contributed to this book and helped facilitate pictures, words and more. Specifically, the folks at Right Brain Brewery, Northern Natural Cider House, the Traverse City Senior Center and Traverse City Roller Derby. Also on this list are past National Cherry Festival president Denny Braun, Traverse City Area Public Schools' teacher Sue Kelly, past National Cherry Festival queen Kelly Plucinski and Belle Photography's Dan Dinsmore.

Acknowledgements

Lastly, but most importantly, thanks to my lovely wife (and roller derby superstar) Lisa Kelly, who encouraged me every step of the way and who put up with many a text that said something akin to "I'll be at the History Center until about 7:00 p.m." after leaving at 7:00 a.m. that morning for my awesome day job at Interlochen Center for the Arts. Thank you for putting up with that, me and handling those little kids of ours through the times when I should have been there taking over. I love you, mami!

INTRODUCTION

Welcome to the National Cherry Festival, ladies and gentlemen! I'll admit, this journey that you are about to take through the festival's history and the stories that go along with it, as well as the discoveries you are about to make, is a journey that I took for the very first time while writing this book.

The Library of Congress has this to say about what it holds in its archives regarding the history of our very cherry (and very long-running) event: "Documentation includes a catalog providing a festival pictorial history, with a focus on Cherry Festival Queens; a picture book about Traverse City, the 1999 festival guide, a calendar, and a magazine article."

I sincerely hope that this book lives up to the expectations of those associated with the festival and pumps up that Congressional collection a bit.

I knew all about the festival as it now exists before I dove into this tome. I knew what I liked and what I didn't like, where I wanted to be and what I wanted to avoid. I knew the events, the rides, the food and the drink. I knew my modern festival inside and out. But I did not know *the festival*.

As I dug into the history of the National Cherry Festival, I discovered its almost century-old roots, its well-earned spot in history, the way in which it wove itself into the fabric of this city and the vital marketing tool that it was to the farmers of the region.

Digging deeper, I found that it was a festival on the cutting edge of history, unafraid to tackle hot-button issues, all while maintaining an enviable neutrality while storms surged around it. The festival always was and always

Introduction

Cherry Festival queen Carolyn Hazzard and her court cut quite a massive cherry pie. This pie appeared in the 1933 parade.

will be this way, despite the best efforts of some who have no idea with what they attempt to tinker.

I also followed the festival through tragedy and saw how its own brand of escapism helped to heal a wounded nation. I watched the festival in a time of war bring a bit of "back home" joy to troops that may never see home again.

I came to know this National Cherry Festival for much more than its concert stage, its beer tent and its Ferris wheel. I saw that it was a living, breathing beast whose life force was the community that supported it.

I followed the festival on a journey that saw it rise from a one-day, laid-back affair costing a couple thousand dollars to put on to its present-day offering: nine days at a budget approaching $3 million.

From its humble roots to its current, iconic incarnation, I followed it. And now, I humbly bring it to you.

I am certain that I have missed a name or three, and that some date that should be is not. This is by no means an exhaustive retelling of every National Cherry Festival moment to ever occur. It is a story of a community's celebration, how it grew and how it became the thriving, much-loved, worldwide phenomenon that it is today.

This is the story of your National Cherry Festival. It is ever changing and ever growing. I sincerely hope that, with a bit of knowledge, this book also plants a bit of wonder.

This amazing, outstanding thing is happening in the streets, shops, restaurants and open spaces of Traverse City, Michigan. And it is there for everyone.

The celebration of a simple fruit. Who knew it could be so grand?

Chapter 1
FROM LOG TO CHERRY

It all began with $4,500. That is the amount paid in 1852 by the Hannah and Lay Company to one Captain Harry Boardman for the purchase of the good captain's lumber mill and two hundred acres of land. Some of that two hundred acres included a small Northern Michigan burg within the county of Grand Traverse.

That's right, folks. Perry Hannah bought our beloved vacation paradise of Traverse City for just over $4,000. Granted, that $4,500 in 1852 is the equivalent of approximately $150,000 today, but still, that is a grand bargain by any measure!

In those days, lumber barons ruled the North. In 1881, as Traverse City was being incorporated into a village by an act of the Michigan state legislature, the grandest baron of them all, Perry Hannah, further cemented his legacy in the hearts and minds of Traverse City dwellers for all eternity as he easily won election as the first village president. In 1895, he further secured his role in Traverse City lore by being elected the first city mayor, a position he occupied for nineteen years.

This town's forefather's presence is still very much felt to this day. One can tour his palatial home, now the site of the Reynolds-Jonkhoff Funeral Home, and visit his likeness in parks and buildings. It is abundantly clear that lumbering was very good to this man, many around him and the region.

But this business of logging was short-lived. According to historical records, lumber boom towns rose and fell all around Traverse City. Mass comings and goings were common. These left behind them ghost towns and clear-cut forests.

But Traverse City was different. The land lent itself to something more than a simple clear-cut and move along. There was a bit of magic present in the soil.

In 1878, an intrepid farmer set about planting massive swaths of cherry trees on the Old Mission Peninsula. By 1888, dozens of farmers had followed suit.

These original farmers took advantage of the unique location, climate and surroundings of the Grand Traverse region. The proximity to Lake Michigan and its various bays made for grand temperature moderation. The leveling of extreme temperatures by the lakes and bays prevented damage to the trees by way of winterkill or to the fruit by way of spring frosts. The rolling hills provided excellent sites to ensure air drainage when cold weather occurred, and the long northern winters provided the dormant period necessary for the cultivation of deciduous fruit.

In short, these farmers looked about them, saw the perfection that existed for this crop and put that perfection to use.

In fact, as far back as 1870, the nation was reading about the desirability of the Grand Traverse region's fruit growing climate. It was during that year that the *Atlantic Monthly* wrote:

> *It is well known to all who have given special attention to meteorological phenomena that the blighting winds which prevail during the earlier winter are those from the southwest. It is equally true, but perhaps not so generally known, that the blighting affect of these winds is always greatly mitigated when they sweep over large bodies of water before striking land.*
>
> *It will be seen that the southwest winds must sweep the whole length of Lake Michigan before striking the shores of the Grand Traverse Region and we find the same rule in force here as elsewhere in regard to its affect upon climate and vegetation. Apples, cherries, pears, plums and all of the best varieties of vegetables attain their highest degree of perfection in this favored land.*

Strong words, no? Even though the early days of farming in the region saw farmers utilize the potato as their base crop, every farmer had their plots of mixed fruit, and every farmer favored those plots above all else.

After the final bits of logging industry faded away, cherries were there to pick up the slack. B.J. Morgan set up the first cherry processing plant in

Traverse City, and the Leelanau County Cherry Home Canning Company set up shop as well. The Cherry Home Canning Company utilized the natural waterways both for shipping processed fruit and for transporting the lugs of freshly picked cherries to a plant in Northport.

Before that, BJ had begun experimenting with growing fruit trees. He discovered that red tart cherries (the kind one finds in grandma's homemade pies) were particularly productive in the porous, sandy soil and climate that had so nourished the massive trees that the lumbermen had chopped down. From that discovery came industry.

As this industry grew, Traverse City soon became number one in the nation for tart cherry production, with Leelanau County sitting at third. The entire region became home to the highest concentration of sweet cherries in the Eastern United States.

By the early 1900s, the production and shipment of cherries was well underway. While the shipment of fresh cherries had virtually stopped by 1912, the manner in which cherries were to be preserved and shipped was beginning to take shape. By 1922, the Grand Traverse Packaging Company was freezing cherries at the point of production, at first without sugar, but then later with. Sugar helped with the preservation of the flavor, color and texture of the cherry.

It is also interesting to note that by 1922 an annual gathering to bless the blossoms had been around for about a decade. Little did these farmers know the amazing beast this laidback affair would soon become, but I digress.

These advances in shipping, mixed with the perfect cherry-growing apparatus that is the Grand Traverse region, saw a true boom of sales and profit during the decade that spanned 1920 to 1930. Plantings of cherry crops increased greatly throughout the region during this time. It was clear to all that the cherry was king in Grand Traverse.

Of course, growing a cherry is no easy feat. The cycle of the cherry year was a tremendous gamble for the growers. These farmers faced winterkill, spring frosts and pests galore. The cherry may have been king, and its profits may have been grand, but this king was a frail and fickle one, a fruit in need of a blessing.

It was with this need in mind that, in 1923, the combined churches of the Grand Traverse Bay region were asked to pray for the success of the harvest. Out of this request came the more formal Blessing of the Blossoms ceremony, which was held on a Sunday in May when the cherry bloom was at its peak. A more organized celebration of the cherry had begun.

The National Cherry Festival in Traverse City

The National Cherry Festival was begun as a literal "Blessing of the Blossoms," as seen here during the festival's earliest days.

A car decorated and ready for the inaugural 1925 Blessing of the Blossoms Festival.

This prayer, held among the blossoms on a warm spring day was the precursor to a massive celebration that every Michigander, as well as many more from across the nation and world, knows and adores.

This prayer begot unto us the National Cherry Festival. (Please forgive that bit of bible-slanted language there. It just seemed to fit.)

In 1925, the first hints of what we know now as the National Cherry Festival came about, thanks to an enthusiastic community and one Edwin E. Eikhoff, the recreation director for Traverse City. Eikhoff gathered together an action committee after a date of July 4 had been chosen for the festival, a date that was chosen as it landed squarely within harvest time and, of course, coincided with another grand celebration. The action committee consisted of the city's F.P. Boughey, the canners' Don Morgan and the growers' C.G. Sherwood. As with any grand tradition, this one had a bit of a rocky start, not the least of which was a money gathering issue on the side of the farmers, who had agreed to contribute one penny for every tree in

The National Cherry Festival in Traverse City

The 1926 Blessing of the Blossoms Festival queen and her court pose for a quick photo before leading the festivities.

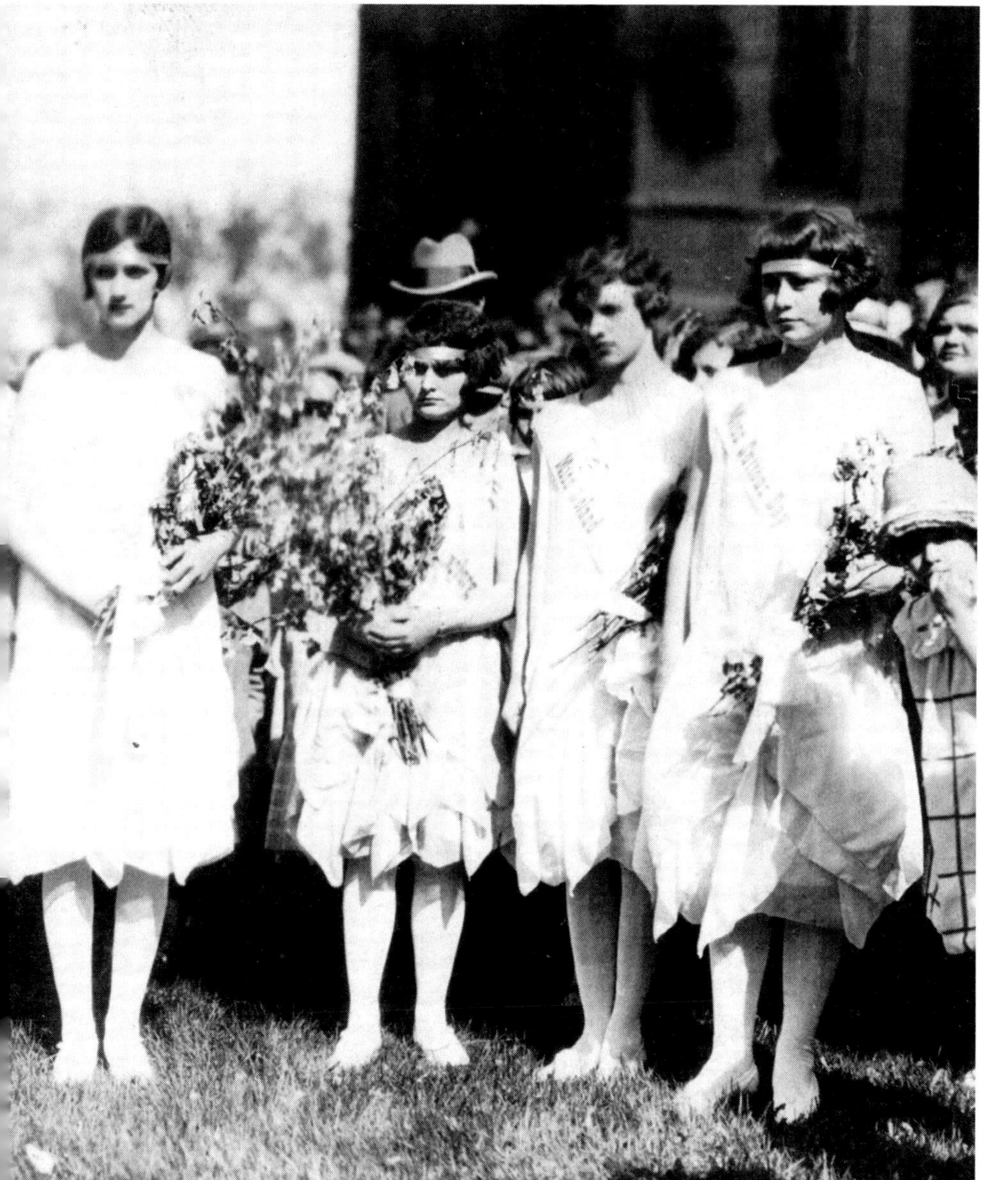

their orchards but had contributed near nothing. This failure to garner cash lead the *Traverse City Record Eagle* to proclaim the Cherry Festival dead and laid the blame for that death squarely at the feet of the farmers.

Still, as local resident and community leader Jay P. Smith had declared, something needed to be done to attract tourists to the Grand Traverse region. Mr. Smith is credited by some sources as being the creator of this Blessing of the Blossoms Festival. Whether that be fact or not, one thing remained: this region needed tourists to thrive, and now that Henry Ford had given the nation a way in which to easily travel over long distances, this region needed to figure out a way to put wheels on the road, bound for Traverse City.

The festival founders insisted that the way in which to attract folk from across the state was laying before them, almost killed off by bickering and politicking. So the project moved forward, and the festival was not dead after all.

On May 22, 1925, the very first Blessing of the Blossoms Festival took place. In a semiformal manner, the people of the Grand Traverse region gathered together to celebrate the rich harvest of cherries and its resulting dollar amounts.

The celebration lasted only a day and consisted of a parade, athletic games, marching contests, a community picnic and the coronation of Queen Gertrude Brown of Traverse City. Three thousand people attended this celebration.

Serving as general chairman was the editor of the very newspaper that had declared the festival dead, *Record Eagle* editor Jay P. Smith. Smith's chief assistants were Leo P. Kalahar and Michigan Transit Company ship line manager George M. Johnson. Orchardist Harold Titus also played a major role in ensuring the overall success of this first festival, as did the local Rotary and Kiwanis clubs, which had guaranteed the expenses the month prior to the festival.

This first festival held some rather amusing bits and pieces, at least to those of us looking back on it today. Chief among those bits would be the queen process. Entries were unrestricted, the only rules being that the nominees must be local and photogenic, as the event would be filmed. The honorable Fred H. Pratt drew Gertrude Brown's name out of a hat, making her the first Cherry Queen. Brown was crowned by Mayor James T. Milliken after taking part in the "mile of beauty" (as described by the *Record Eagle*) that was the grand parade. The parade featured brass bands, marching groups, Spanish-American and World War I veterans, horseback riders, clowns and fifty-two floats.

While all of the festivities were held among the surroundings of downtown Traverse City, the actual blessing took place atop the Friedrich Tower, built by shoe store owner A.V. Friedrich, which stood forty feet tall and was positioned on Center Road (the Old Mission Peninsula's main drag) at its highest point. The Reverends William Chapman and Demas Cochlin gave this first official blessing.

It wasn't too long before Mr. Smith and his festival cohorts realized that a May festival meant that children weren't yet out of school, making family travel difficult. So the organizers swiftly moved the festival to July.

It wasn't long until news got out about this northern party, and in 1928, the state legislature, recognizing the event's importance to the region and state, designated this gathering with the moniker "National Cherry Festival."

Thus was born a legend. A behemoth. A moneymaker. A much-loved tradition.

Thus was born our Cherry Fest.

Chapter 2
CHERRY EXPLOSION

"COME TO MICHIGAN!" cried a 1929 Chicago paper advertisement. "Come and join with thousands from all over the country in making merry during the National Cherry Festival. Three days of parades, pageantry and revelry, glorifying Michigan's famous Cherry Harvest!"

This ad goes on to discuss the many other activities to distract you as well, including the fact that one can fish for trout, bass, pike and Mackinaw trout and do some deep water fishing as well. But really, come for the cherries and headquarter at one of the hundreds of summer hotels that line Lake Michigan.

Despite the slightly confusing marketing message, folks were coming to Traverse City in the thousands. They came for the beaches, they came for the outdoors, they came for the escapism and they came for the cherries.

Despite the fact that 1927, the third year of the festival, saw a bad crop and thus no festival, the cherry was firmly ensconced as the Traverse City trademark. By the 1930s, Michigan governors and senators, as well as presidents, vice presidents and high-ranking military personnel, were meeting, mingling with and crowning glamorous Cherry Queens galore. Chief among those was 1930's Signe Holmer, eighteen, of Manistee. Queen Signe was the epitome of cool. She wore a countenance that would befit any actual royal, a bit aloof and obviously aware of her beauty. A flapper-esque sort, she was sent straightaway to Washington, D.C., to hand off a cherry pie to President Hoover and to New York City, where a rough landing destroyed the pie meant for mayor Jimmy Walker, who was plenty gracious nonetheless.

Some young, dapper folks enjoying the downtown festival scene during the 1920s.

It certainly was no small feat for a festival that had barely reached past its fifth year to be sending its queen to meet the president or hearing its state governor, Chase Osborne, proclaim, "Eating cherries is going to make for a stronger mankind."

In spite of all this, questions began to crop up (no pun intended) surrounding the exploding production empire that surrounded the cherry.

"Production is fast reaching a figure which will threaten an over supply for established markets," stated one 1932 cherry industry article. "In the year 1920, five million pounds of cherries were produced in the United States. In 1928, 69 million pounds were marketed, and Michigan, with forty million pounds, took the lead as a cherry growing state."

The cherry explosion had most certainly begun.

That same article estimated that 3.3 million sour cherry trees had been planted in Michigan in the span of less than a decade. The author asked if such growth is sustainable from a profit perspective. The article also questioned supply, demand, farmer output, input and gain. It certainly did question a lot.

But to the folks at the National Cherry Festival, such questions were moot. Times were good, and the festival was booming.

Indeed, these booming times continued throughout the 1930s and into the '40s. This time of boom was no better represented than by the good Governor William A. Comstock during the Governor's Ball in 1933.

Blessing of the Blossoms

Time for pie!

A mainstay in every festival parade are our veterans, as seen here with a World War I veterans' float from the 1920s.

The National Cherry Festival in Traverse City

You see, this governor had sworn during his campaign that he would not be indulging in the frivolity that is crowning queens. There was far too much state business at hand, and he would, no doubt, be far too busy for such trifles as queens and crowns.

The 1933 National Cherry Festival was happy to change his mind and open his eyes a bit as to what these frivolities, and the symbols that they carried, truly meant to the state, especially this thing called cherry.

"I had no conception of the magnitude nor importance and significance of the National Cherry Festival until I viewed the one now underway," he said during his speech at the Governor's Ball.

No worries, the festival seemed to say, you would not have crowned her anyway.

In fact, there was a certain lady set to lay the crown on Morella Oldham's head that year. Eleanor Roosevelt had been invited to crown the queen but was unable to make the event. She sent Senator Arthur Vandenberg in her stead, and Governor Comstock looked on as the good senator placed the crown.

Needless to say, Mr. Comstock was a one-term governor. Turned out crowns and queens weren't all that trifling after all.

A grand example of that came the year before, in 1932, when Queen Carolyn Hazard flew to Washington, D.C., to deliver a cherry pie to President Hoover. Once that delivering was done, she made the short trek over to the National Broadcasting Company, where she gave a speech that was broadcast coast to coast. It was a grand speech, and thanks to the *Ludington Daily News*, we have the exact wording of it.

Queen Carolyn said:

> *Do you remember that old song "Can You Make a Cherry Pie Billy Boy, Billy Boy"? Well, that's what we're singing and whistling up in Cherryland in Northern Michigan now in anticipation of the National Cherry Festival, to be held in Traverse City, Michigan on July 14, 15 and 16. Our National Cherry Festival may seem just like another celebration to you radio listeners, but up in the heart of the Grand Traverse cherry land, it is far more important than that. It symbolizes the advance of the army of pickers on the cherry orchards and the whir of machinery in the packing plants. This land of Northern Michigan is one that you should all see with its hundreds of sky blue lakes and miles of sand beaches all buried in green forests. We hope that someday, everyone of you listeners may join with us in our Cherry Festival with its floral and juvenile parades, our air maneuvers, the exhibition drills by the Coast Guard, and all of the other things which go to make up our celebration. We want you to come up and celebrate with us, for up in Cherryland, life is just a bowl of cherries.*

A 1935 postcard depicting the queen's float.

Queen Carolyn certainly had a way with a microphone. And her message seemed to stick.

By 1934, the National Cherry Festival was setting attendance records, not the least of which were the eighty thousand people who lined the streets of downtown for the "big parade."

The year 1935 brought in a bit of corporate influence, as Traverse City was witness to its very first sky writer, who scrolled "Chevrolet" into the clear blue summer sky.

Throughout this decade, queens were rubbing elbows with presidents and the Hollywood elite, crowds were growing, the calendar of events became a booklet and the cherry continued to be an incredibly sought-after device, as did the National Cherry Festival.

In 1938, the *Ludington Daily News* proclaimed that "this city broke out in gay array today in preparation for the National Cherry Festival." Chamber officials estimated that around 100,000 people would roll into Traverse City for the festivities that year.

The paper went on to describe that the queen for that year, Josephine LeFranier, who would arrive to launch the festival on Wednesday morning, riding the Coast Guard cutter *Escanaba*. She and her court would be escorted

The National Cherry Festival in Traverse City

Marching on Front Street, circa 1936.

by a fleet of eight naval training boats, marking the first time that Traverse City was literally invaded by the Cherry Queen.

That last bit was my own, not the papers. But, to be fair, thanks to the National Cherry Festival, everyone wanted a little piece of Traverse City.

A less-than-lighthearted association between the festival and the coming World War would come in the previous year, 1937, when that year's National Cherry Queen, Eileen Lyon, was crowned by the ambassador to the United States from Japan, Hiroshi Saito, who was himself embroiled in a large amount of warring scandal as his nation went to war with China. Not long after this crowning, the ambassador passed away and was carried home with honors by the USS *Astoria*, a United States Navy Astoria class heavy cruiser. This gesture, made in 1939, was intended as a show of gratitude for an almost identical gesture that the Japanese had made in returning the body of U.S. ambassador to Japan Edgar Bancroft on the Japanese cruiser *Tama* in 1926.

Upon arrival in port, and following the lavish state funeral, the Japanese showered lavish hospitality on *Astoria*'s crew.

It was in October 1939 that the *Astoria* was reassigned to Pearl Harbor. However, when the infamous date of December 7, 1941, came about, the *Astoria*, while still assigned to and stationed at Pearl Harbor, was seven hundred miles from Pearl Harbor with Rear Admiral John H. Newton's Task Force 12, which was acting under orders from Admiral Husband E.

Kimmel, commander in chief of the Pacific Fleet, to reinforce Midway and Wake Island, as his suspicions had been piqued by the mounting tensions in the Pacific. But as a result of the Japanese attack on Pearl Harbor, that reinforcement mission was cancelled, and the fleet was ordered to patrol an area southwest of Oahu with instructions to intercept and destroy any enemy ship in the vicinity of Pearl Harbor.

Astoria would soon welcome aboard around forty sailors from the battleship *California* who had survived the attack on Pearl Harbor. And the circle, it seemed, was complete.

But that circle, save for the association between one queen and her crowner, was now nearly half a world away from the much-lauded and sought-after National Cherry Festival.

So sought after was the festival and its host city, in fact, that it was used in a bit of politicking. In 1941, the queen's crown fell upon the head of Christine Michels. She hailed from farther away than any other queen ever had. In fact, she hailed from farther away than most of the festival's attendees.

Queen Christine was the daughter of Rodolfo Michels, the Chilean ambassador to the United States and a very good friend of Senator Arthur Vandenberg. And Queen Christine wasn't the only Cherry Monarch with a somewhat real-world royal connection.

The 1940 National Cherry Queen was Barbara Brown of St. Ignace. She was crowned by Michigan congressman Albert Engel. However, she stated that she was disappointed that her father, Prentiss M. Brown, was unable to attend the crowning. You see, he was busy at the National Democratic Convention in Chicago where Prentiss, otherwise known as U.S. Senator Brown of Michigan, was being propped up by his friends and colleagues for a potential run for president. This did not end up coming about. But Senator Brown enjoyed a very successful career in politics thereafter and, in 1951, was named chairman of the new Mackinac Bridge Authority, a position he held until his death in 1973.

National and international politics, pomp and circumstance, power plays and golden days. This was the National Cherry Festival. It seemed that it was finally, and firmly, ensconced in the region's collective tradition and that nothing would end its reign.

Then, all of a sudden, something did.

World War II broke out, and the nation didn't feel much like celebrating. Efforts were turned toward conserving and providing for the war effort. Men marched off to war, and the region's mighty women stepped up to work the fields and the orchards.

The National Cherry Festival in Traverse City

A postcard depicting the crowds on Front Street following the big parade.

One perfect example of this is Sandra Petertyl. When her father, Willard, left to enlist, Sandra gathered her friends together and recruited them to help save the region's cherry harvest.

"With more than 50,000,000 pounds of cherries ripening and half of the harvest already contracted by the U.S. Government to feed the armed forces, Sandra said she wanted to make sure that her dad gets all the cherry pie he wants," wrote one local publication. "Besides these girls, hundreds of office workers and home folks who never worked in the orchards before have volunteered their services. More than 12,000 workers are now plucking at the heavily laden trees."

From 1942 to 1947, the National Cherry Festival lay dormant, gathering dust, awaiting the moment that war left the world and a bit of carefree abandon was once again OK.

The year 1946 came and went. The festival committee deemed that date too soon after the end of the war to hold the festival. The next year, 1947, brought the Traverse City Centennial Celebration from June 29 to July 4. While this celebration was officially branded the "Traverse City Centennial and National Cherry Festival," the celebration focused on the centennial more than the cherry.

The centennial did host a cherry pie–eating contest, air shows, music and much more, but this certainly was no Cherry Festival.

Michigan governor Mennen Williams waves to the Front Street crowds.

There was, however, an overabundance of beards. A kangaroo court was set up to find and "punish" beardless men; grand parades and contests surrounded these beards.

Questions were asked: "How does a man shave?"

Questions were answered: "You don't. You don't shave. That's how a man shaves."

The love for beards and centuries lasted but a year. By 1948, queens (locals only, decided Traverse City) and cherries ruled yet again.

The festival of 1948 lasted only two days, July 8 and 9, but those two days were a grand return for the festival.

"After having been packed away in moth balls during the war years, the National Cherry Festival is being taken out of its package this year, polished and brightened for its revival on July 8th and 9th in Traverse City, Michigan," read an announcement letter from the National Cherry Festival board.

Upon its suspension in 1942, the festival was the fourth-largest event of its kind in the United States.

1949 Cherry Festival queen Ann Mauer picks cherries in a promotional picture for the festival.

"The South has its Mardi Gras, the Pacific Coast its Tournament of Roses and the Middle West its National Cherry Festival," the letter continued.

The festival was back with a bang; of that, there was no doubt. The city commission renewed its ordinance that no desserts other than cherry desserts be served at any establishment during the festival. More than 250,000 people crowded into Traverse City, a town of 15,000 permanent inhabitants. Of those 250,000 people, the festival estimated that one in every four carried a camera, meaning that images of the festival would be spread out over at least fifty thousand homes. Oh yes, this fiesta was back.

The year 1949 saw a bit of verbal change enter the cherry vernacular. The first use of the terms "tart" and "sweet" to describe the two very distinct forms of cherry was witnessed, forever saving housewives and wee little ones the shock of tart when all they wanted was sweet. Men couldn't taste anything but beard at this time, so they didn't care much what the food was called.

The year 1950 saw a grand celebration. In fact, even Mother Nature seemed to revel in the harvest celebration this year.

Blessing of the Blossoms

1951 Cherry Festival queen Mary Lonn Trapp receives her crown from Charles Figy as the 1950 queen, Joyce English, looks on.

"Weather befitting a Queen prevailed today as pretty Joyce English sailed into port to preside over the 25th National Cherry Festival," wrote the *Owosso Argus Press*.

Traverse City had just turned one hundred, and now the National Cherry Festival was turning twenty-five. This year's festival was billed as the "25th Silver Anniversary of the Cherry Festival." New on the roster for this year was the location of the queen's coronation. No longer would this take place at Clinch Park. This year, Queen Joyce English became the first royal to receive her crown at Thirlby Field, courtesy of Michigan's secretary of agriculture Charles Figy. Figy placed the crown on the queen's head as some six thousand spectators looked on and cheered. Figy was quite the mainstay in cherry queen crowning, in fact, even continuing in that role after he left Michigan to become an assistant U.S. secretary of agriculture.

The cherry crop of 1951 was outstanding—too outstanding, in fact. A labor shortage necessitated what may have been the first large-scale use of immigrant laborers to help in the harvesting of cherries. Five hundred

The National Cherry Festival in Traverse City

The ever-popular Budweiser Clydesdales.

1955 Cherry Festival queen Sharon Dolan and her court at the beach.

Liberace served as the theme for this mid-century festival float.

Mexican nationals were flown in to provide this help, being paid nine cents per pound of red tart cherries. Records continued to be set this year. Over 125,000 spectators lined the streets of downtown for the grand parade.

A grand tradition that went on for some time was born in 1953 when Anheuser-Busch sent its famous Clydesdales to take part in the festivities. They set up camp in the Waddell Buick garage on State Street. One and all were invited to come and view them free of charge.

Throughout this festival's history and into the festival of today, you will no doubt notice that most events are free of charge. This is certainly no accident or oversight. This is a festival of the people, as they say, and it continues in that vein.

The year 1957 was a grand illustrator of that "of and by the people" mantra, as it featured a seven-mile-long grand parade, witnessed by over 100,000 spectators.

By 1958, even aliens were aware of this earthly celebration, or so some thought. On the last evening of the festival, folks reported seeing a flying saucer racing through the skies. None of these folks were festival goers, however, as their eyes were all trained on the closing fireworks display at 9:30 p.m., when the sightings were happening. As it turns out, the National Observatory reported that the rocket that had launched Sputnik II into space was visible for a time in the Western skies. Who knows, though? Cherries may be an interplanetary treat as well!

In 1959, the glorious worlds of pancakes and cherries met head on as Aunt Jemima (yes, *that* Aunt Jemima) was the featured guest of honor, hosting a pancake breakfast at the American Legion Hall. I doubt more American of a sentence has ever been written than the one that you just read.

Americana was indeed rife at the festival. It was steeped in it, based on it and enveloped by it. It was a community celebration unlike any in the nation, and it drew numbers to this small northern burg in a way that nothing else ever could have or ever had before. Change was most certainly on the horizon, but this festival had weathered a World War and the better part of a decade without any celebration. This festival had done that, and on its return, it was bigger and it was better and most certainly just as popular, if not more.

Oh yes, change was coming, but this was a festival that was built for change.

Chapter 3
THE FESTIVAL GOES NUCLEAR

It appears to have cost around $20,000 to put on the National Cherry Festival in 1963. If you were to flip back to that original chapter (otherwise known as Chapter 1), this sum is approximately four times the amount that Perry Hannah bought the entire region for.

One might recall an old saying: "As General Motors goes, so goes the nation." Well, in its own way, throughout its history, the same can often be said for the National Cherry Festival and the Grand Traverse region: "As the Cherry Festival goes, so goes Grand Traverse."

Many folks who pick up this book will, no doubt, be fans of minutiae. Well, allow me to indulge those folks for a bit here in 1963.

True history buffs will know that 1963 is the year in which the infamous George C. Wallace took the governorship in Alabama, the *Mona Lisa* was exhibited in the United States for the very first time, the Beatles recorded their debut album, Alcatraz closed, the first James Bond film hits theaters, President John F.

Governor Williams waves from yet another convertible.

1963 Cherry Festival queen Mary Kardes receives her crown from 1962 queen Geri Schmidt.

Kennedy gave his *"Ich bin ein Berliner"* speech in June and was assassinated in November and, of course, much, much more.

For the folks putting on the National Cherry Festival in 1963, it was a stellar year. Modern Cherry Festivals have suffered through heat, but not too many in recent memory have topped the one-hundred-degree mark, like this one did.

It was a pivotal moment for the queen as well. For the first time in over thirty years, contestants were accepted from outside the Northwest Michigan region. This year's queen, Mary Kardes, hailed from Lansing but summered with her family in Williamsburg, a short drive from Traverse City. Queen Mary, along with newly elected governor George Romney, 120 floats and many other drill units, equestrians, marching bands and the like, took part in the grand parade despite the sweltering temperatures.

Now for some fun minutiae!

According to the Department of Labor form #6233217-5F, fifteen- and sixteen-year-old girls were paid $1.00 per hour to promote and publicize the National Cherry Festival. The National Cherry Festival paid $305.55 to the West Michigan Tourist Association for its yearly membership. It also paid the Rokos Drug Store $366.83 for makeup used by mummers (a sort of clown entertainer). That year's Governor's Breakfast cost $474.95. The queen and her court were clothed for $3,028.09. Frank McManus was paid $3,103.01 for five lugs of cherries. Miss Leelanau was put up at the Sundown Motel for $8.32. The Muller Baking Company was paid $40.76 for pies to be used in the pie-eating contest.

Obviously, many more such records exist, with amusing or interesting ones being available in the hundreds. But you get the idea. This 1963 festival was a very different beast from the one in 1925.

Indeed, the festival of 1965 ran for five full days, with the festival's official agenda spanning nine days, including July 4 activities and post-festival events. This was quite a booming bit of growth as 1962's festival spanned only two days.

Agenda items in 1965 included a "Deb-On-Aire" Dance at the Park Place Motor Inn from 9:00 p.m. until 1:00 a.m., with a $1.00 cover charge, on July 4; the National Cherry Queen talent contest, also held at the Park Place and also with a $1.00 cover charge, on July 5; tours of Grand Traverse region orchards on July 6; the Queen's Ball with a whopping $2.00 cover charge on July 7; a plethora of band concerts on July 8; the Youth Parade (with Disneyland in Cherryland as the theme) and an air sea rescue demonstration by the Coast Guard on July 8; a water ski show, more band concerts, the Governor's Breakfast (apparently the governor didn't pull them in like the queen did, as his cover charge was only $1.50) and the Grand Floral Parade on July 9; and the National Cherry Festival Concert, hosted at Interlochen Arts Academy on July 10.

Obviously, the above is nowhere near to a complete listing of events—simply a highlight—but even in this highlight, one can see that the National

The National Cherry Festival in Traverse City

1963 Cherry Festival queen Mary Kardes with Michigan governor George Romney.

Cherry Festival was, at the very least, showing signs of the dominant entity that it was becoming in the region.

By 1968, the region was producing around 100 million tons of cherries. This worked out to be approximately one-third of the world's supply of cherries. While many years' crops from Northern Michigan were damaged by severe weather, local cherry farmers held strong and continued to produce cherries in amounts that kept Michigan top-of-mind when cherry production was the topic.

Even in 1968 (the year that the festival was officially christened a weeklong celebration), the National Cherry Festival was boasting around 200,000 (300,000 in 1967, according to the *Record Eagle*) attendees during its now six-day run.

"Starting modestly as a purely local celebration of the annual cherry harvest, it has attained international importance as a fiesta," wrote the *Record Eagle*.

A grand line, that: "attained international importance as a fiesta." That sounds like a very important party. So important, in fact, that folks were walking 160 miles to get here for the festival!

According to the *Owosso Argus Press*, it was in 1968 that three long-distance walkers had completed a 160-mile hike to Traverse City and took part in one of the festival's parades. Those walkers were Fred LaVene, seventy; and Marion Pearson and Earl Robson, both sixty-nine.

At this point in the festival's history, it was launched with the arrival of its queen and her court. This kicked off a "celebration of fun and activity including contests, concerts, parades, orchard tours, a carnival complete with midway, dancing in the streets and the friendly greetings of people having fun," so, again, wrote the *Record Eagle*.

The *Record Eagle* continued: "The whole festival is climaxed on the final day by the Grand Floral Parade, breathtaking with its gorgeous floats, when the Queen bestows her smile on her thousands of subjects lining the parade route, and by the Mummers Parade later the same evening, when fun is king and joy is rampant."

National Cherry Festival lovers of today may not yet fully recognize their beloved fest. With words like "mummers" and "Grand Floral Parade" being tossed about, this certainly doesn't seem to be any festival that you might recognize.

Well, 1967 is about to begin to remedy that for you. It was in that year that the National Cherry Festival organization announced that the Grand Floral Parade would henceforth be known as the Cherry Royale.

The organization explained that the change was made "in keeping with the desire of the National Cherry Festival to place more emphasis on the product which the Festival honors—Michigan Cherries."

Despite this edict, 1967 also brought with it some very unfamiliar cherry-related fun.

First and foremost among these bits of fun was the Rajah's Lost Crown. According to the *Detroit Free Press*, the crown, valued at $25,000

Marching band members relax in Clinch Park after the 1975 parade.

and belonging to a "world famous Treasure Chest collection" owned by jeweler Meyer Rosenbaum, contained 687 diamonds, emeralds and sapphires set in gold filigree. This crown supposedly belonged to some long-lost rajah. Rosenbaum graciously loaned the crown to the National Cherry Festival, which, in turn, gave it to festival president David Pearce, who refused to actually crown 1967's Queen Linda Kaye Christie. Pearce held the crown above Queen Linda's head for a few moments and then gave it to her to hold as she made her way off stage. Indeed, judging by the deep crease left by the crown on the *Detroit Free Press*'s Roslyn Boccia's head, the crown's ten-pound weight was simply too much for anyone to bear for too long a time. This assumption was further backed up by Louis Tamarkin of Meyer Jewelry.

"It's purely ceremonial," he said. "It couldn't be worn, it's just too heavy."

That year, Queen Linda was warned to not enter India, "at least, not wearing that crown, anyway."

Another bit of fun was had at the fairgrounds that summer. The Seabees, in an effort to celebrate their twenty-fifth anniversary, decided to set off a nuke—well, demonstrate such a thing on a small scale, at least. Local papers described the scene like this: "A scale village was wiped out by a simulated nuclear blast on July 13 at Grand Traverse County Fairgrounds. The blast, scaled and carefully controlled, was designed to flatten some of the buildings and to burn others to the ground. This was followed by an 'enemy' attack. This is a training exercise for the Seabees and to stimulate interest in civil defense."

Of course! Why not? The Cold War was raging. What's more fun that watching a simulation of what everyone feared would actually happen?

Finally, it wasn't just the festival that was creating strange and unique bits of fun; many interesting brands and ideas were springing up around the festival in an effort to gain from the festival's popularity.

A grand example of that would be the thirty-three families who hit the road, traveling from Mount Pleasant. They traversed via horse-drawn wagon. This wagon train was made up of around 150 people, 110 horses and nineteen horse-drawn wagons. The group took the back roads on a 130-mile trip to Traverse City. The sponsors of this event were the Chippewa Wranglers Riding Club. Scouts were sent ahead to plan the route, food and provisions were set out along the way and trial runs were made. At the end of this ride, the families stayed for a bit in Traverse City and, you guessed it, enjoyed a bit of cherry pie.

The 1960s were good to the festival and Traverse City. It was during this decade that articles and other recognitions began popping up touting Traverse City as a fascinating and beautiful destination in and of itself. In the August 1967 issue of *Better Homes and Gardens*—a behemoth at that time, enjoying a readership of more than seven million—Traverse City was listed as one of its "10 Most Fascinating Cities" in the nation. While the National Cherry Festival took top billing in the reasons why Traverse City fascinated them, the magazine also mentioned the Con Foster Museum, the Duncan L. Clinch Yacht Harbor, Grand Traverse Woolens, the Maud Miller Hoffmaster Art Gallery, the House of Flavors, the Pinestead and more. Slowly but surely, Traverse City was rising in its own right.

But, as ever and always, the National Cherry Festival reigned. It was in the 1960s that the festival seems to have truly come into its own. Looking back now, it seems rather obvious that such a thing would happen in that decade. A positive omen popped up in 1960, when Murrie Tompkins took the crown as cherry queen. Queen Murrie was the daughter of 1938's Miss Mancelona Rebecca Mavety, a member of Cherry Queen Josephine LaFranier's Court.

Along with that connection came 1960's Miss Greilickville Carole Green (there were an awful lot of Misses back then). Green was the daughter of Ethel Kroupa, who had held the Miss Old Mission crown in Queen Josephine's court. Further, Ethel Kroupa came from a very prominent cherry-farming family, one who had played a major role in establishing the region's cherry dominance. Oh yes, the signs and omens abounded that year. The '60s were going to be good!

The year 1961 saw a rather humorous parade happening when a tradition was established that would span most of the decade. Two Arabian horses, Zietes and Raansaane, were named Grand Floral Parade marshals. This tradition would carry on through 1966 in some way, shape or form. M.E. Gray of Manistee, or Eddie, as folks called him, owned Lake Bluff Stables. It was from Eddie's stables that these grand marshals would come. And so, for six solid years, either Eddie (in 1964 and 1966) or a selection of his horses served as grand marshal. Soon enough, however, people tired of this tradition, and the grand marshal sash was quietly returned to the human race full time.

In 1964, the festival committee, having decided in 1962 to scale back celebrations from three days to two, saw fit to expand the celebration to a full five days. Governor George Romney dutifully proclaimed the week of July 6 "National Cherry Festival Week."

The year 1965 saw further growth of the festival as the Cherry County Playhouse (or the Cherry Players, as some might remember them) was moved from under a tent in the parking lot of the Park Place Hotel and into the Park Place's newly built Park Place Dome. This new theater in the round offered seating for seven hundred and further cemented the fact that the festival was thoroughly in the midst of a heyday that showed no signs of slowing.

By 1968, the National Cherry Festival was officially a behemoth. It ranked comfortably among other fests such as Mardi Gras, the Tournament of Roses, etc. Evidence of this is offered up by the queen program, which began accepting applications from all over the state, as a proper statewide and nationally renowned festival should. The first queen to be chosen from a statewide pool was the tall, blonde bombshell Julie Ann Hamilton.

The year 1969 saw the precursor to today's Cherry Roubaix bicycle race. City athletic director Vojin Baic thought it a very good idea to organize a ten-mile-long bicycle race. Sixty-seven others agreed, and in the end, Don Basch finished first with a time of twenty-eight minutes and twelve seconds.

BLESSING OF THE BLOSSOMS

Michigan governor Milliken greets young parade watchers.

The festival was adding, promoting and growing at a rapid pace by now. Its board of directors consisted of sixteen members, and its presence was solidified on the national stage by the slogan: "A pretty little town, a tasty little fruit, a folksy little celebration. My, how they've all grown!"

This bit of PR was the understatement of the decade, if not the century.

The '60s was yet another decade of growth and change for the festival. The decades that lay ahead promised more of the same. Another war was in full swing, the nation's values and priorities were shifting and those in the midst of that shift needed respite and reprieve. The National Cherry Festival was ready to provide just that.

It was in the 1970s that the National Cherry Festival really began to look and feel like the festival we know and love today. Bits and pieces that today's festival goers might recognize made their way onto programs and events calendars.

But before that could happen, the festival went to Vietnam.

Chapter 4
THE PRESIDENT ARRIVES

Queen Barbara Beckett had quite the year between 1969 and 1970. Not only was she rubbing elbows with Chicago mayor Daley and taking part in popular television variety shows, like the *Bob Braun Fifty Club*, she was also demonstrating that the cherry's reputation as the "nation's fruit" wasn't just a marketing ploy.

"Traverse City's 1970 National Cherry Festival also will be celebrated in far off Da Nang, South Vietnam, the NCF office announced today," proclaimed the *Traverse City Record Eagle*:

> *The China Beach USO at Da Nang, serving some 60,000 GI's a month, has told the Festival organization it wishes to take part in this year's July 6–12 Cherry celebration and the NCF is taking steps to give all the assistance it can.*
>
> *Decorations for the USO are being provided by the Red Cherry Institute, the NCF is sending information to those planning the Da Nang event, and National Cherry Queen Barbara Ann Beckett of Traverse City is to record a tape for each day of the Festival, to be sent to South Vietnam along with an autographed photo of the Queen.*
>
> *In addition, the NCF is asking for community wide aide in assuring the success of the Da Nang celebration.*

The article goes on from there, detailing the ways in which the National Cherry Festival would be shipped overseas, split in two, all to benefit "the

The National Cherry Festival in Traverse City

boys" in Vietnam. Cases of cherries, cherry pies, décor and more were sent to Da Nang, where, mixed with the dulcet tones of the queen's recordings, they allowed the soldiers a bit of respite from the quagmire that was Vietnam.

From a USO publication:

> At the China Beach USO in Da Nang, National Cherry Festival Week was celebrated with a bang—brochures, programs, flags, and photos of the Cherry Queen were used as decorations. These had been sent by Mrs. Dorothy L. Walkmeyer, Director of the Festival, which is held every year in Traverse City, Michigan. Best of all, delicious homemade goodies, which had been baked by the citizens of that community, arrived and were rapidly consumed. The men loved them, as it brought a touch of home. Activities at USO China Beach included a Cherry pie eating contest, Cherry picking contest, and dart game. A floor show followed these events.

"All the boys were so happy and cheering when they mentioned Traverse City," says Eugene Farkas, then a marine from Charlevoix. "I was very happy to hear that they were going to celebrate the Traverse City Cherry Festival over there.

"I went to a big USO event and they had a sign up saying 'If you're from Northern Michigan, come to the office,'" he continued. "When I went in, they asked me if I had ever heard of Traverse City. I said 'Why sure, I live not too far from it and have relatives there.' Turns out they got a letter from the National Cherry Festival office with information on the Cherry Festival. They planned to celebrate it in Vietnam at the same time that Traverse City celebrated it, and they wanted to take my picture for attending the celebration of National Cherry Festival week."

By this time, attendance at each festival was easily topping 375,000, the calendar of events had turned into a multi-page booklet and Hollywood stars lead the grand parade. In fact, in 1971, Buddy Ebsen, of *Davy Crockett* (and much more) fame, rode high on a sporty blue piece of topless Detroit hardware, as did *Mayberry RFD* star George Lindsey in 1972, and in 1973, Duke Ellington visited the National Music Camp at Interlochen (now known as the Interlochen Center for the Arts, also the Interlochen Arts Camp during the summer) to perform with the camp orchestra. Interlochen and the festival have quite the history together, in fact, with Interlochen hosting a concert in celebration of the National Cherry Festival's closing day for some time.

A beautiful shot of the grand parade in 1975.

Another huge part of the National Cherry Festival's entertainment scheme was the Cherryland Band Classic, one of the largest band competitions in the Midwest. Bands would travel from all over the nation to compete in this affair. Some had no problem finding money for the trip, while others had to get a bit creative. For example, one band sold twenty tons of potatoes in order to be able to afford the trip.

All this entertainment and the festival had quite an impact on the local economy, much like it still does to this day. In 1972, the festival was credited with pumping over $9 million into the region's economy. Quite a number, that!

So desirable was the festival, in fact, that in 1972, the *Ludington Daily News* wrote, "You might keep in mind that the conditions that make an area ideal for Cherry production are the conditions that make an area ideal for vacationing. A gentle climate, picture book scenery, inland lakes and rivers well populated with fish, miles of warm sand beaches and air cooled and cleansed by the waters of Grand Traverse Bay are some of the many attributes of the area."

A somewhat less entertainment- and vacation-minded topic was also broached at the 1972 festival, one that got right to the soul of humanity. Strangely enough, this topic was discussed in San Antonio.

The *San Antonio Express* wrote:

> *Involvement of ethnic minorities in all phases of big festivals and celebrations is a must if the festivals hope to last very long. That's the word from two festival experts who are in San Antonio this week for a four day [sic] national convention of the International Festival Association. About 60 delegates from 40 major festivals throughout the United States are attending the sessions at El Tropicano Motor Hotel.*
>
> *In an interview Monday, the association's president, Mrs. Dorothy Walkmeyer of Traverse City, touched on some of the problems and trends of big celebrations across the country. She said that part of the spirit of any successful celebration is that "it's the community working together, not just one social group, but every element of the community." She said today's festivals must be in tune with changing trends and needs.*
>
> *One such area, she noted, is the "connotation of queens for festivals." Mrs. Walkmeyer, who has spent nine years as managing director of her city's National Cherry Festival, said the trend is away from queens for celebrations. "Young people object to the queen connotation because they feel they were chosen in beauty contest kind of competition and for the wrong basic reasons," she said. Mrs. Walkmeyer said that festivals retaining queens go for "more contemporary" approaches, moving away from the image of a promotional queen who "is delicate, says the right thing at all times and cannot have any of her own thoughts and certainly not able to contrary to the establishment." She said the new look in festival queens is toward girls chosen for their intelligence and personality.*
>
> *Another problem touched on by the association president and its public relations coordinator, Bob Shoemaker, was the question of participation by ethnic minorities. Shoemaker, assistant manager of the Festival of States in St. Petersburg, FL, said a festival "must be a mirror of the population or it won't be around very long."*
>
> *Mrs. Walkmeyer said the inclusion of ethnic minorities in festivals has been particularly evident in big cities where there are large minority populations. "This will eventually shift down to the smaller festivals," she added.*

It certainly does seem rather strange to read those words in today's Traverse City, where so many mix and mingle without a care for one's ethnicity, but as with many other bits and pieces of national history (such as the national race movement), this area, and its festival, were right there on the cutting edge, leading the way toward what a festival for and by the community should be.

While this leadership took place, outstanding personalities continued to make their way to Traverse City. In 1973, the festival saw Soupy Sales star at the Cherry Country Playhouse in *Come Live With Me* and almost saw Colonel Sanders himself glide through the grand parade route. He had to cancel at the last minute due to illness but was nonetheless still quite prominent in the festival's program. Lucien Pierre Ginoux, a prominent French winemaker and guest of Senator George McManus, took the good colonel's place. In later years, this winemaking business would come to rival the cherry for regional dominance. But, for now, wine was a part of Traverse City's somewhat distant future. The cherry yet reigned supreme.

Interesting side note, while on the topic of winemaking: The year 1974 saw the Schlitz Beer Company's forty-horse hitch team of Belgian horses pull a Schlitz-branded circus wagon, four horses abreast and ten rows deep, down Union Street, the current home to such iconic Traverse City beer houses as 7 Monks (which highlights Belgian brews) and Brewery Ferment. This, too, was a bit of an omen, as the hop and microbrew have become Traverse City staples as well.

Moving on from such refreshing things as that, we catch back up to the cherry.

The year 1973 saw the National Cherry Festival undertake its very first public service project, and like the beer bit you have just read, this undertaking was to be a bit of a predictor of things to come.

These days, Traverse City is well known as a bike-friendly community. In fact, with each new street project and biking season, a new bit of cycling-friendly trail or area seems to be added. Little did Mrs. Bea Noye, the festival's 1973 director, know that when she penned her letter of April 12 to a Maryland newspaper, she was making Traverse City history and influencing future Traverse City law and guidelines as well.

She wrote the *Observer* to say that the festival was working on a campaign to put an "entire city on bicycles." She listed parking shortages, gasoline shortages, air pollution, improved health and saving money—from parking fees and taxes to support new lots—as reasons behind this push to pedal.

April 25 was to be the first free biking safety class, conducted by the city police department and the director of city recreational activities. This was to be followed by a "big kick-off parade" on April 30, led by then First Lady of Michigan Mrs. Wm. G. Milliken and the National Cherry Queen Trudy

The National Cherry Festival in Traverse City

Yarnell. Schools were allowing any student who wished to take part in this ride to be excused for the day, and many local businesses were lined up and ready to take part.

"We are aiming our publicity primarily at downtown store employees who drive only a mile or so to the downtown area and park their cars for 8 to 9 hours," said Noye. "But, we are including any student, housewife, or anyone interested in our ecology plan.'

She had been working for a solid month with the city police department in an effort to map out safe street routes to the downtown area, as well as spreading the word about cycling safety and the rights of cyclists.

"We believe if other towns and cities would popularize bike riding, as it is in Europe, we would all be better off," she said in a letter. "I have been riding while our plans progress and find it just terrific, and 50 years is all I confess to in age. So, everybody out!"

Another fine example, of many, wherein the festival found itself on the edge of a soon-to-be popular movement.

What's that? You want another example of the Cherry Festival taking on the global scale of things? Well! The year 1973 also saw a bit of savvy cherry marketing as a result of a sixty-day price freeze on cherries. Governor Milliken urged growers to take the majority of their 82 percent of the national cherry crop and market it overseas, where the prices were higher, thus saving the nation from higher fruit prices in other popular fruits, such as apples and blueberries. This would have come about as a result of the farmers' attempting to recover massive financial losses on their cherry sales. Quick thinking, that!

Now back to the fest!

The festival of 1974 was predicted by the *Argus Press* to be the largest in the festival's forty-eight-year history. The big cherry harvest celebration is considered one of the top festivals in the country and annually hosts more that 350,000 during its event-packed six days, the paper wrote.

But thanks to one very big appearance, the 1975 festival would blow away that of 1974.

It was in 1975 that the National Cherry Festival received some very special guests. In that year, the *Ludington Daily News* wrote:

> The program for this uniquely family oriented event is prepared and served like a superb, giant Cherry pie, with a slice for everyone, from the toddler to the octogenarian. For 49 years the Cherry harvest has been celebrated in Traverse City by a Festival which is now one of the major

President and Mrs. Ford make their way through downtown Traverse City as part of the biggest lineup of parade floats in the festival's history.

> *events in the country. The fine area recreational facilities, the beauty and the charm of the countryside, the hospitality of the people and the excellent accommodations of all types have added to the popularity of the Cherry fete.*

First among the guests who were about to enjoy that legendary local charm and accommodation was Queen Helen Boughy (the festival's very first queen), who, after an "18 or 20 year" absence from the area, made her return to the Grand Traverse region and its festival. Now known as Helen Nolan, she made the trek from San Diego to Traverse City to visit with family. She said that when she won her crown, beauty pageants had barely even been heard of at the time, so she was reluctant to take part in the queen selection. But after three community leaders—Don Weeks, Loren Bensley and Carl Pratt—spoke to her about the program, she agreed to give it a try and "everything turned out fine."

Secondly, after years of trying, broken promises and folks sent in their stead, the National Cherry Festival finally landed a president, in the form of Michigan's own Gerald Ford.

The presidential team arrived in typical fashion. Menacing men cased the streets, and tanks made to look like cars traversed them. But as often was the case with President and Mrs. Ford, when the actual appearance happened, the mood took on a relaxed, affable sort of style. Indeed, the president and first lady were very much enjoying their time in Traverse City. During a trip to a local orchard to pick and taste sweet cherries, the president wore a plaid sport coat and an unbuttoned, white button-up shirt without a tie. The epitome of relaxed style, of that there is no doubt.

Thus was the effect of the National Cherry Festival. Rather, thus *is* the effect of the festival. Even the world's most powerful man can wear plaid and relax.

But for some, this relaxing was becoming a bit taxing. Complaints were heard of the size of the grand parade in which the president participated. With 180 units, it was simply too large, they moaned. And so, by 1977, the festival's governing body had decided to limit parade entries to 130.

This limiting of the parade participants proved to be somewhat fortuitous, for it was in that year that the July heat shattered all of the records. In fact, a few members of bands competing for the John Minnema Memorial Trophy at Thirlby Field passed out from heat exhaustion and were whisked via ambulance to Munson Medical Center, where they came to in air-conditioned comfort.

But for a few coldhearted folks, this 1977 festival seemed to be the last straw. Grumblings began to grow. The festival was almost fifty years old by now; hadn't it had enough fun? Surely we don't need 300,000 people traipsing through our lovely hamlet year after year for an entire week! Was it all really worth it? Did it all really matter that much? It's just a dumb ol' cherry, after all…

"It takes a tremendous lot of history to make a tradition," said Henry James, who spoke his mind much in the way the majority of folks would have spoke their mind had the *Record Eagle* asked them to, as it did him. "The Festival is a special tradition that's a product of a special area that is attached to its past, proud of its present and dedicated to maintaining its stature and future."

Over the coming years, the tide would ebb and flow on this anti-festival quibble. Too much would turn to too little. The festival's profit and loss margin would be called into account. This or that would upset some "get-off-my-lawn" type, and yet, the festival would keep on. For as many came to learn, and many still learn and know today, the National Cherry Festival is woven into the fabric of this community, whereas one's lawn, or one's abrasive personality, certainly is not.

Chapter 5
BIG HAIR AND THE ARNOLDS

In 1978, the festival saw the beginning of a long-standing and much-loved tradition; one that would see the ever-popular United States Navy's Blue Angels become a semi-annual custom. But first, the air force came to town. The United States Air Force brought its impressive Thunderbird team to town, making a most impressive showing with the T-38s, putting on a thirty-minute show that attracted thousands of spectators to the shores of West Grand Traverse Bay.

The Blue Angels, which would soon become a staple of the festival, thanks to the opening provided by the Thunderbirds, which were themselves festival staples for a time, are the second-oldest flying aerobatic team in the world, behind only the French Patrouille de France, formed in 1931. The Blue Angels were formed in 1946. Nowadays, the Blue Angels fly F/A-18 Hornets in more than seventy shows around the world, along with support aircraft, including the ever-popular transport plane, *Fat Albert*, a U.S. Marine Corps C-130 T Hercules that comes equipped with a rocket-assisted takeoff mechanism. On an every-other-year basis (save for a short hiatus due to sequestration cuts in 2012–13), these fighter jets pierce the sky above Traverse City, providing even more Americana and magic to the atmosphere that surrounds the Cherry Festival.

A highlight of today's festival is always the extensive people-watching opportunities. One can find such watchers relaxing at sidewalk bistros, on the beach, on front porches and more. In 1978, a humorous quote appeared in a local newspaper, attributed to former deputy sheriff Bill Box of Kingsley,

The United States Navy Blue Angels make quite an entrance.

who came out of retirement every year to help with festival traffic. The eighty-year-old lawman hadn't missed a festival in thirty years. He said that many things had changed in those years with the festival, one of which was the dramatic change in lady's beachwear.

"It seems that just two handkerchiefs will do it these days," he said. "And, old as I am, I still appreciate it."

Folks in the know will tell you that the Bayside Festival Stage hosts some outstanding entertainment every festival week, offered up by some very big names in music. The year 1979 gave a hint of what was still to come in the festival's future when the festival hosted superstar Debby Boone. Debby was in town for a whirlwind engagement that saw her rehearsing, interviewing, sound checking, singing songs (including her hit "You Light Up My Life") and then hopping back on the road. What a life for that twenty-two-year-old daughter of Pat Boone!

A pretty common occurrence took place at the 1979 festival when the Fourth of July landed on a weekday. For many communities throughout the state and nation, this could cause a bit of a headache for folks who wished to celebrate but had to figure out the best way in which to celebrate midweek. For those residing in or visiting Traverse City, this problem was, once again, moot, as the entire region was already deep into celebrating the fruit that George Washington made famous and would do so for days after the national holiday.

"God bless the Cherry Fest," many thought as they stretched out their blankets on the sand or grass to take in the show.

The year 1980 rolled in with another hot week of Cherry Festival fun and fancy. The crowd that gathered to watch the Grand Royale Parade was upward of 150,000 and more, the second-largest parade crowd in the festival's history.

"There was a lot of people along Front Street," said city police lieutenant Richard Johnson. "But, back when Ford was here, you couldn't even see the pavement."

In 1981, there was a pretty drastic change in the way in which the queen was selected. In years gone by, the queen was chosen in late June after a competition. Now, the field of twenty-one was narrowed to six by festival time through a series of interviews. Those six were then carefully observed throughout the festival and then chosen on Friday evening at the Cherry Royale Queen's Ball at the Grand Traverse Hilton in Acme, just in time for the new queen to make the winding ride through town in the Cherry Royale Parade the next morning. While some felt that this diminished the queen's role in one way or another, others agreed that the overall goal of the queen program was two-fold: one, to empower a young woman with the spoils of victory—scholarships and such—and the second to promote the region's cherry industry. The queens weren't in it for the celebrity, although quite a bit of that came along with the crown as well.

The next year, 1981, also brought a bit of religious controversy to the festival, care of the Moonies. It seems that several downtown businesses were met with visits from representatives of the Unification Church, otherwise known as the Moonies, during the week of the 1981 National Cherry Festival. Members of this church were referred to as "Moonies" because of the church's founder, Sun Myung Moon. These representatives chose a path that Jesus probably would not have chosen were he at the 1981 festival, in that they entered downtown businesses seeking donations (a violation of local ordinance) and told those who chose to donate that the monies were destined for the festival, not their Moonie bank accounts.

"One of them walked in here, too," said Dorothy Newman, the festival office manager at the time. "I asked him if they had a permit, and he stammered and stuttered and slid out the door."

This was not the first time that Moonie pride had taken form on Front Street, however. In 1980, some members of the church, whose MO was to hand out flowers and ask for cash, collected money on behalf of the Northwestern Michigan College's Technical Center. And by that, they of course meant their church, not the college at all.

As luck would have it, 1981 also saw Krishna Consciousness in the streets, passing out literature and soliciting funds. A banner year for "out there" religions was 1981.

It was also a year in which the National Cherry Festival made a few changes that modern Cherry Festival visitors may recognize today. The Cherry Royale Parade was officially moved from Friday afternoon to Saturday morning, as was the 15K race. The queen's coronation took place toward the end of the festival at a gala ball instead of during a pre-festival event. Bed races made their first appearance, in a rather "zany" way; a cherry ice cream social was established; and an area of the festival was set aside for the serving of cherry-based food products throughout the day.

More cherry, same community focus. That was this changed festival in 1981.

The 1982 festival saw the streets melt in the heat, literally stopping the parade while marchers gathered their shoes together from the sticky tar and road workers scattered sand to allow them to continue.

Heat turned to star power in 1984 as Willard Scott led the big parade home. He was an enormous hit with the crowd. His antics, humor and charm won over one and all.

The '80s carried on as only the '80s could, full of large hair, larger personalities and large amounts of fun. The National Cherry Festival was beginning to show signs that it wasn't just a tradition, a yearly party, something that would come and go. Oh no, this mighty festival was beginning to look like exactly what it was, a piece of Traverse City that would always be there. As long as there was a Traverse City, as long as there was a cherry, there would be a Cherry Festival.

Part of that "large fun" of the '80s began in 1982 when a young entertainment firm known as Arnold Amusements would first occupy the midway.

"The National Cherry Festival is honored to have at its midway attraction in 1982, The Arnold Show," read the flier announcing the new partnership that lasts to this day.

It continued:

Ivan Arnold had a dream, and he's making that dream a reality. Arnold, owner of Arnold Amusements, the major amusement company at the National Cherry Festival, has wanted to own his own carnival and play his hometown of Traverse City and his dream came true. They travel all over Michigan, but coming back to their hometown is quite an honor.

Arnold and his wife, Agnes, are both Traverse City natives, as well as their three children, Tom, Sandy, and Jon, who all graduated from Traverse City Senior High School. Ivan believes that it's important to present a good image by keeping the rides neat and clean, along with the help, clean and in uniforms. Besides providing a clean atmosphere, the Arnolds say their priorities are to give folks a happy glow and a good time. After all, the lights and music and smiles are replicas of the world they love. They describe their own life as a "carrousel" [sic].

Along with this amusement institution, another institution was being honored in 1982: George McManus Jr., who was honored as Cherry Industry Man of the Year.

Throughout the '80s, the queen's hair got bigger, more color made its way into festival photographs and Vice President George Bush ate cherry pie, courtesy of Queen Cindy Pleva.

The National Cherry Festival in Traverse City

In 1983, it was "Cherries, Cherries and more Cherries!" according to the *Milwaukee Journal* as it touted the festival within its pages. With another decade almost in the books, the Cherry Festival was as strong as ever and even more popular to boot.

"Open Wide and say enter me in the Chef Pierre National Cherry Festival Sweepstakes!" So screamed the headline of an ad spread by the good chef and his company before the 1985 festival:

> *Time to celebrate the Cherry with traditional favorites like Cherry pie from Chef Pierre. And where does Chef Pierre find those Cherries—so juicy, so red, so plump? Right there in our own hometown, the Cherry Capital of America, Traverse City, Michigan. That's where you'll be headed if you win the National Cherry Festival Sweepstakes. Grand prize is a trip for two to the National Cherry Festival. You'll fly, expenses paid, to Cherry Capital Airport. Have a Cherry red rental car at your command. And enjoy a stay in one of the country's most charming resort communities. You'll be guests of honor for five days of festivities, highlighted by the Cherry Festival Parade. Plus, you'll receive $5,000 spending money while you're there! Or, win one of 100 first prizes—free Cherry pie for a year. Or the second prizes—500 official Cherry Festival cookbooks.*

This ad came with a coupon for twenty-five cents off your next Chef Pierre pie.

Oh, what one could do with $5,000! That could buy you a lot of cherries in 1985. Apparently, it was a very good year.

One thing was amiss, however. It seems that Charleyoix had the bigger pie.

It was true. Charlevoix, Traverse City's neighbor to the north, held the record for largest cherry pie. In 1988, the National Cherry Festival decided that such a thing was unacceptable and set about changing the record books.

The festival did just that on July 25, 1988, when a twenty-eight-thousand-pound pie was baked and displayed at Traverse City's Open Space. This pie beat Charlevoix's record by a whopping fourteen thousand pounds. In true Traverse City fashion, residents had seen the challenge, and they had doubled it.

People began showing up at 5:00 a.m. to witness the record being set. When it was all over, more than thirty-five thousand people were handed seven-ounce cups of pie after the pie was judged, cut and served.

Pie filling ingredients included 18,865 pounds of cherries, 7,478 pounds of sugar, 966 pounds of flour, 855 pounds of corn starch, 117 pounds of vegetable oil and 45 pounds of salt. The crust consisted of 1,081 pounds of flour, 703 pounds of shortening, 286 pounds of water, 32 pounds of salt and 54 pounds of dextrose.

The pie was baked in a brick oven constructed at the Open Space. A pie pan measuring eighteen feet wide from rim to rim and twenty-six inches deep was made for the pie and was lifted into the oven via crane.

All of those cherries in that huge pie seemed a bit lavish come 1989, when a fungus invaded area orchards. According to the *Ludington Daily News*, an already small harvest was suffering the affects of an invading fungus. The paper wrote that the U.S. Department of Agriculture said that Michigan's red tart cherry harvest, already suffering from 1988's drought, would be 70 million pounds, down from 1989's 110 million pounds. The American Agricultural Marketing Association predicted an even smaller harvest for 1989, coming in at 63 million pounds. These predictions did not take into account the affects of the fungus.

"It's the worst I've seen since I've been around and it's my 14th year in cooperative extension," said fruit pest expert Jim Nugent at the time, when asked about the leaf drop fungus plaguing Northern Michigan's cherry harvest. The fungus is titled as such because its signs and symptoms include a spot growing on the leaf until the leaf drops off the tree. Leafless trees are unable to collect and build up nutrients for the winter and for the following year's growth.

Despite this concern, the trees were not overtaken, and the cherry harvest would bounce back with overflowing orchards full of cherries in the decades to come.

Again, everything was big, from hair to pie to cherries on the vine! But even with the largeness of the '80s, nothing could really compare to what was to come. The most recent decades of the festival are the time in which it came into its own, fulfilling the hopes and wishes of those who founded it and those who ran it over the years and continue to run it. This people's festival, a celebration of a simple, delicious fruit, was about to meet the '90s and then cross that bridge into the new millennium. And soon, it would take its full shape as the National Cherry Festival that we all know and love today.

The awkward '90s still lay between the Cherry Festival and now. A time of peace and prosperity in the nation as a whole would see the Cherry Festival grow even more, add on even more and become even more well known, attracting visitors from all over the globe.

As global transit became more accessible to the "common man" and it was no big deal at all to buy a ticket for a plane, this festival of ours would find itself on a global stage, the center to so many vacation plans.

The National Cherry Festival in Traverse City

This tiny little thing that began so long ago, with a simple priest, a parade, a picnic and games, has grown into a marketing and fun-creating behemoth. And it was nowhere near finished growing.

Onward to the '90s, because we all adore the smell of teen spirit!

Chapter 6
OUR MODERN FESTIVAL

Queen Elizabeth Gertz led the festival into the last decade of the twentieth century. And what a decade it would be!

During that decade leading up to Y2K, the real Sara Lee paid the festival a visit; Cherry Dollars made a rather short-lived debut; fighter jets buzzed the beaches; wild animals roamed the streets (courtesy of visiting circus folk), including the ever-popular Laura the Elephant, a baby Egyptian elephant; glasses got big; shoulder pads exploded; Spencer Christian (of *Good Morning America* fame) did his weather report from Traverse City; Vince Gill charmed the lady folk; Governor John Engler pushed his brand-new babies down Front Street; Ringo Starr and Clint Black rocked the town; folks complained that a tiny speck of a building located on the city's no longer open Open Space was ruining their view of the bay, while ten feet away stood the massive light-and-power plant, a true obstruction by any means; a wise Grand Traverse Zoological Society board voted "No" on a proposal to place the festival's beer tent next to the buffalo enclosure at the city's zoo and inside the mini-train tracks (nothing good would have come from that mixture, to be sure); the "chair chaining" tradition—wherein one can reserve their front row seat at the parade—was severely limited, with anyone leaving a chained chair downtown more than a couple hours returning to their chairs and finding a bright orange notification of a fine or no chairs at all; and much, much more.

In fact, no. We'll continue this run-on sentence! It's an awful lot of fun.

Two famous beards rocked the main stage during the '90s (ZZ Top), Miss White Lightnin'—one May I. Wettcher-Wissle—gracefully road atop her convertible in the big parade, Cherry Queen Kelli Kaberle held Jay Leno's cue cards, Reba McIntyre and Bonnie Raitt rocked as well (minus the beards) and mountains of cherries were consumed, along with countless pounds of cherry pie. Beaches were full, bands marched, people came, sand sculptures were raised and the National Cherry Festival turned seventy-five.

The year 1991, in which the festival turned seventy-five, saw an estimated 500,000 visitors decend on the Grand Traverse Region—an increase of 497,000 over the very first festival. To say that the festival was enjoying success would be a severe understatement.

The *Toledo Blade* wrote, "Even though hotels and restaurants are as busy as the Festival, don't assume you can't get a table at great spots."

Indeed, although many savvy vacationers had standing reservations for National Cherry Festival Week from year to year, the region that surrounded the festival was growing quickly, and the world was taking notice. Downtown Traverse City took on a focus that would lead to the current "local and organic" mindset and practices on display throughout town today. Folks the world over began to read about more than Traverse City's cherries. The natural beauty of the area was trumpeted alongside the growing food and restaurant offerings, as well as a burgeoning wine industry that would soon come to rank among the world's best. Craft beer was yet to make the scene, but the growing and expanding entertainment options were beginning to take shape, as was the local arts movement as well. All of these things would soon take shape and mature into what Traverse City is today—a veritable Mecca for anyone seeking a beach, great music, outstanding nightlife, entertainment galore, some of the best local food anywhere and a brew and wine scene to die for.

Ah yes, soon the National Cherry Festival would not be the only game in town. And, to be honest, that was perfectly OK with the folks at the Cherry Fest. It was something they had been wanting for some time. This incredibly beautiful region was becoming a year-round destination, not just a place to be for one week out of the year.

But there were still a few folks who didn't quite grasp that concept yet. A rather amusing statement was written within the pages of the *Argus Press* when, in 1993, it stated that Traverse City had its fifteen minutes of fame when national television network cameras visited from ABC and CBS. Never mind the fact that the festival had been attracting hundreds of thousands of visitors from around the world for many decades now. Little did these *Argus Press* folks (and anyone else spouting the "fifteen minutes" malarkey) know that Traverse City was in the midst of a renaissance that would see it become one of the most sought-after vacation destinations in the world.

But, again, I digress.

"It invariably happens that when people see something that they like, they'll remember it come vacation time," said *Good Morning America* producer Kevin Magee.

When *CBS This Morning* came to town that same year, Cherry Festival directors sang "Oh, What a Beautiful Mornin'" for some reason. They also interviewed a cherry farmer and the winner of a Taste of Cherries contest. Also, as you read earlier, ABC's weatherman Spencer Christian gave weather reports from Traverse City for both *Good Morning America* and *World News This Morning*.

According to the *Press*, *Good Morning America* also taped a segment on the Rotary Charity here in Traverse City, at that time the richest Rotary Charity in the world. The Cherry Royale Parade was also broadcast live across the Midwest.

Bryan Crough, then executive director of the Downtown Traverse City Association, mentioned that the region had also benefited greatly from mentions by NBC weatherman Willard Scott.

What is it with weathermen? When did they become so chic and world-traveled? What about the weather?

Speaking of things that can't be controlled, this fruit that the National Cherry Festival celebrates can be a fickle beast. Some years, it is overflowing with plenty, and the celebration takes on the joy that echoes outward from the orchards themselves. And then there are years like 1995.

According to the *Toledo Blade*, there was little celebrating among cherry growers on the eve of the 1995 fest. Prices were driven to a mere fraction of the actual cherry production cost.

"I can't even afford to harvest them for what I'm going to get," said Harold Edmondson at the time. Edmondson's orchard is a mainstay among area orchards and had been in operation for decades by 1995. "Our best bet is to put them on the ground and hope the good Lord helps us out next year."

The *Blade* stated that Edmondson and his fellow growers would be participating in the 1995 festival but that participation would be somewhat less than celebratory.

Jim Nugent, a specialist with Michigan State University's extension service, said that tart cherries that year would be selling for around five cents per pound at wholesale markets. At that time, the cost of producing and harvesting Cherries was around twenty-five cents per pound. The farmers were taking a huge hit in 1995.

According to Nugent, the 1995 cherry market was made even less attractive by the fact that around seventy million pounds of Cherries from the 1994 harvest were still sitting around, frozen, nationwide.

Michigan remained an incredibly dominant force in cherry production, with the U.S. Department of Agriculture stating that 320 million pounds of the total 391 million pounds of cherries produced in the nation would come from Michigan in 1995.

"We're king of the hill where tart cherries are concerned," said Nugent to the *Blade*. "But cherry growing runs on boom and bust cycles. It looks like this year will be a bust for consumers."

The year 1998 brought a touch of tragedy to the National Cherry Festival as a privately owned military jet disappeared. This jet, a Czech-built L-39 Albatross, left Traverse City's Cherry Capital Airport for a practice flight before it was to be showcased in that year's National Cherry Festival Air Show. The search for the missing jet was suspended after three days by the Coast Guard. Michigan State Police and a cadre of volunteer pilots continued searching, however, in the Fox Island area. The plane's early origins were based in training Russian pilots.

The pilot of the missing jet was identified as Don Schaller, with the plane's other occupant being Don Rodriguez. Schaller was a member of the

Red Star Squadron, a Quincy, Illinois–based group of individuals who buy planes from the former Soviet bloc for display at air shows and other events. Rodriguez had been a flight instructor at Traverse City's Northwestern Michigan College since the 1970s.

After the L-39's disappearance, the Russian MiG-21 that was to have appeared with the L-39 during the air show was grounded, and that part of the performance cancelled. However, the Blue Angels still put on a display.

Strangely enough, this plane and its two occupants have yet to be recovered as of the writing of this book in 2014. The Michigan State Police hold that the plane most likely went down in what is popularly known as the Great Lakes Triangle, an area of the Great Lakes that has more unexplained disappearances per unit area than the Bermuda Triangle. A bit of sad mystery for that century's last decade.

A similar incident, without any mystery, was honored during the 2001 Cherry Festival, when local United States Air Force pilot Captain Mitchell August Bulmann ejected from his stricken aircraft over the Atlantic Ocean but was later found dead by the Coast Guard. The Coast Guard reached the captain less than an hour after the crash, but they arrived too late to save the airman. That year's air show was dedicated to the memory of this Traverse City native.

Examples like these show how this festival is able to handle the joy and the loss all in stride and with an air of elegance not often seen in summer celebrations.

Of particular interest during our current glorious century was 2007, when the cherry crop was beyond bumper. While it is true that some years see very few cherries from Northern Michigan making up the cherry offerings at the festival, 2007 was not such a year.

"We lucked out with the strange weather this past winter and spring," said King Orchards' John King in an *Antrim County Review* article. "We've got a very good crop this year."

According to the National Cherry Industry Administrative Board, 160 million pounds of cherries were had during the 2007 harvest season, a number that was an 11.4 percent increase over 2006.

"One thing's for sure," wrote the paper, "there's plenty of cherries for this year's Cherry Festival."

Speaking (or writing, I suppose) of 2006 and 2007, what was it like running for and being the queen in that year? Well, here's what the *Ludington Daily News* wrote about its hometown girl ("hometown" meaning Ludington) Kaley Lynn Schroeder, who was crowned queen in 2006:

Schroeder will have the week off from fulfilling the duties of Cherry Queen, but her first stop is in Gaylord this weekend and she will continue for almost every weekend for the entire year. During Cherry Festival week, the girls [those competing for the crown] *got to attend concerts and meet country music singer Keith Anderson, they stood on the field at a Beach Bums game, and saw the Blue Angels air show that was in town. Schroeder's favorite part of the week was meeting all of the new and interesting people that she did every day. In the rough schedule that she has received, her favorite things coming up are meeting for lunch with the Governor and a fruits and vegetable show in Grand Rapids.*

A very different view of the festival and the queen selection process came from 2004 cherry queen finalist Sarah Adams. Sarah had made three attempts to gain the cherry queen crown and was part of the Miss Curwood Festival court in 2000.

She made it her goal to at least make the top five finalists list for the 2004 festival. Making that list means that each of the five ladies chosen will wear a sash and crown throughout the festival, participate in all manner of queenly things and generally have as much fun as possible, all while being secretly judged, the most queenly being crowned at the end of the festival to reign as the National Cherry Queen for the next year.

Sarah was on the top five finalist listing in 2004, but her roommate for the week, Maggie Schneider, went on to win the crown.

According to the *Argus Press*, Sarah noted the correlation between the National Cherry Festival and Owosso's own festival by saying that the Curwood festival's format is based on the Cherry Festival's operation. She went on to point out one distinct difference between the festivals' queen programs.

"The National Cherry Queen is a speaking Queen," said Sarah. "It's all about speaking and personality. While the Curwood Festival Queen is a parade Queen. The National Cherry Queen travels all over promoting the Cherry industry."

Despite not winning the crown, Sarah's experience as a finalist was certainly memorable for her.

She said, "We were given an entire wardrobe for the week that we got to keep. The candidates were given an itinerary of what to wear and when. We made three or four clothing changes per day."

She also says that her finalist tiara was a "little tiny thing," but she was very proud to wear it.

As a finalist, Sarah rode in three parades; walked the fashion catwalk; helped select the Queen's Choice car show winner; attended lunches hosted by Kiwanis, Rotary and Elks Clubs; and spoke at numerous events, including Cherry Industry Day.

"Everyday we were up early and stayed up late," recalled Sarah. "It was challenging, tiring. By Wednesday I was very tired, but I kept saying 'this is an opportunity of a lifetime, I have to make the best of it.' And I'd pick myself up and keep going. I knew it would be my last year ever to try out and that it would be back to reality on Monday."

But according again to the *Argus Press*, despite this schedule, there were many perks: signed cookbooks, flowers, balloons from the festival president, her tiara, the $650 wardrobe, a $1,000 scholarship, a sash with her name embroidered on it, businesses' pins for the sash, a nomination bracelet, a professional photo of the Queen's Court and more.

She was also able to sample the local delicacies as well, like cherry mustard, cherry BBQ sauce, dried cherries and cherry-berry nut mix. Lunches, dinners, her hotel room and numerous gift bags all rounded out the local experience. Perhaps best of all, each finalist was able to ride carnival rides and play all of the games for free; and continue to play until each girl had won a prize.

"We'd receive a gift from the Queen every morning," says Sarah. "One day, it was a cherry anklet, the next a cherry toe ring, then fresh cherries. That went on all week. I wrote 56 thank-you notes when I got home."

A less than light topic that has plagued the festival over the years is its avid attempt to stay out of politics, both local and national. Sometimes, this policy creates controversy itself as it attempts to avoid creating controversy—a real Catch-22.

Just such a thing happened in 2003, when the issue of abortion surfaced and attempted to make its way into the parade. The *Ludington Daily News* wrote that an antiabortion student group was denied entrance into the Cherry Festival's Junior Royale Parade.

"I was disgusted, really," said Andrea Becker of Students for Life after she learned of the denial. "We purposely try not to put the word 'abortion' on the sign, and we purposefully tried to avoid the controversy in the first place. They allowed us before, and now all of a sudden they don't."

According to the *Daily News* and the *Record Eagle*, Tom Kern, the festival's executive director, said that the decision was made by a committee of volunteers who review parade applications.

"The Festival is about the promotion of cherries and the community," explained Kern. "We aren't making a statement that these issues are good or bad, but that the Festival isn't the place."

The year 2004 brought a bit of a blemish to the National Cherry Festival's shine as the festival decided to scrap its eight-year-old recycling program, resulting in an additional twenty-three tons of garbage being delivered to area landfills.

"It was too labor intensive and was not being favorably received by festival goers," said festival executive director Tom Kern.

Apparently, this new policy of eliminating the recycling tent and recycling only cardboard was set to save a then financially strapped festival around $9,000. Thankfully for Mother Nature, whom the festival ultimately celebrates, this recycling hiatus was short lived. The festival now has returned to recycling as much as possible.

Another bit of controversy found the festival in 2007 when organizers decided to do away with the Heritage Parade, due to financial constraints.

"The cost structure of putting on the parades and 87 events for free was getting too much to bear," Tom Menzel, festival executive director, told the *Record Eagle*. "We literally did not have enough money."

Of the three traditional parades, festival organizers decided the Heritage Parade was the most logical to cut, but they hope to some day bring it back.

Something a bit more Earth friendly and crowd pleasing is cherry art. Since 1988, a yearly contest has been held to choose whose art would adorn the official National Cherry Festival commemorative poster. In 2012, the winner was David Hodge, a man who had made it his mission to create cherry art in copious amounts. He did this because he was in the process of publishing a book of his cherry art entitled *A Cherry's Tale*. One of those pieces, *Royale Parade*, became the 2012 selection.

David's work is a whimsical celebration of his favorite hometown festival and was chosen from over one hundred entries that year. Hodge, a self-taught artist, took up painting while he was writing a science fiction novel in an effort to flesh out a main character. Hodge decided to bring eighty-six of his paintings to offer for sale at the annual National Cherry Festival Art Fair, in honor of the festival's eighty-six years.

In 2013, a rather oblivious suggestion was made by Traverse City mayor Michael Estes to be rid of pit spitting, pie-eating contests and, yes, even the midway rides. The mayor stated that the festival needed to be more event-driven and that these traditions may have outlived their time.

"A lot of this stuff, I think, the public is getting tired of," Estes told the *Record Eagle* in 2013.

But 2013 Cherry Festival executive director Trevor Tkach said simply, "Hands off."

He surmised, correctly it seems, that these traditional mainstays, and others like them, were true crowd pleasers. And the attendance numbers reflected Tkach's statement.

"I challenge Mayor Estes to a pie-eating, pit-spitting contest any day of the week," Tkach said. "He needs to come down and have some fun with me."

Of course, after laying down the gauntlet, Tkach gave the mayor some props, agreeing with Estes's premise in his statements. Any festival that doesn't evolve with and meet the needs and wants of its people will die, Tkach said.

Part of that evolving happened that very year when Tkach and his team brought the very first nighttime air show to Traverse City.

"I've never seen a night-time [*sic*] air show, so I'm excited to see it, but it will probably be a one-time thing," Tkach told the *Record Eagle*.

Over the coming years, Tkach says that he hopes to increase the festival's focus on health and wellness.

"But that doesn't mean we are getting rid of Gibby's fries and ice cream," Tkach told the *Record Eagle* with a smile. "Everything in moderation."

Our festival is a grand old lady. She has had her ups and downs, her missteps and her setbacks. Yet she soldiers on in the most glorious way imaginable.

The eighty-eighth National Cherry Festival will run officially July 3–12, 2014. While this is a nine-day span, it isn't anything new. When the festival's calendar so closely coincides with the July 4 holiday, organizers expand the festival week so as to encompass the July 4 holiday. At the year of this writing, 2014, the festival was scheduled July 5–12. The decision was made to bump the starting date back to July 3 and to partner with the Traverse City Boom Boom Club (the folks in charge of the July 4 fireworks). This means that if one gets their timing just right, that one (and perhaps a special 'nother) will be able to view the fireworks over West Grand Traverse Bay from atop an Arnold Amusements Ferris wheel. Not too much is better than that! Except for doing it whilst sharing an elephant ear—that would be the epitome of perfection at the National Cherry Festival.

The calendar for 2014 includes many events and activities that folks would recognize if they were picked up from the 1940s National Cherry Festival and placed here in 2014. They'd find the cherry pit spit contest, cherry pie–

The Traverse City Police Department motorcycle unit moves through the parade.

eating contests, the Great American Picnic, Cherries D'Vine banquet, tea with the queen candidates and the princes and princesses, turtle races, a celebration of the cherry connection itself—from farm to table to the fruit itself—Cherry Industry Awards and so much more.

More modern events include a Million Dollar Hole in One Challenge; a Blues, Brews and BBQ Festival; a celebration of film; the HEAT Beach Party; runs; and much, much more!

In fact, this 2014 festival even has a junk food–fighting mascot in the persona of Super Cherry, who is actually mascot of Graceland Fruit. Before his posting as mascot for the National Cherry Festival, he traveled the state touting the benefits of dried cherries. Now, in 2014, Super Cherry's mission has grown to include educating festival goers about the health benefits of cherries and all the ways in which to enjoy them.

According to the festival's website, this Super Cherry, who replaced the retired Mr. Cherry, has quite the origin story.

> *Born of the earth, and burnished by the sun, Super Cherry was grown on a magnificent Cherry tree planted on a towering bluff overlooking Lake Michigan. As the biggest, ripest, sweetest red Cherry in the orchard, Super*

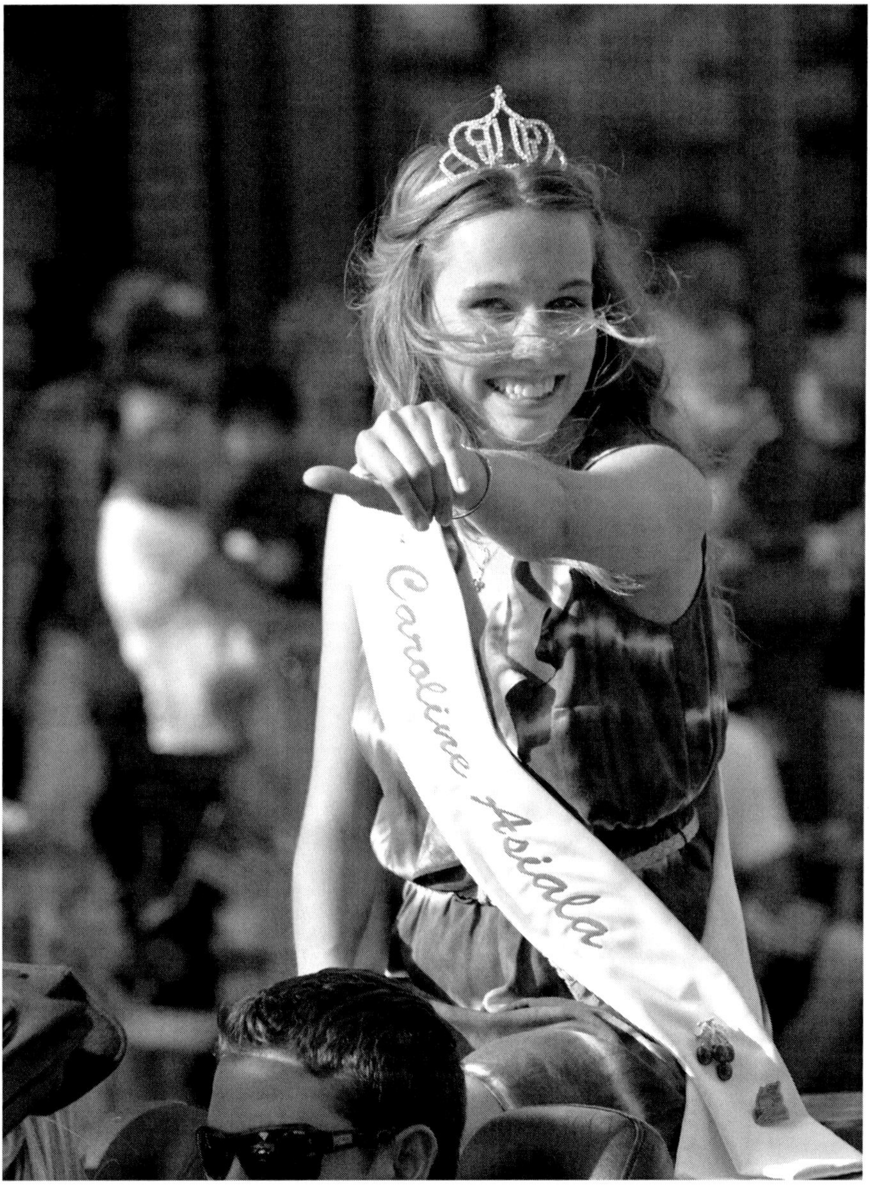
Caroline Asiala

> *Cherry soon realized he had a duty to represent all of his shiny red friends. His mission as Mother Nature's Super Fruit is to help bring the remarkable story of healthy, delicious Cherries to people everywhere. The nice people at Graceland Fruit adopted Super Cherry, and they help connect him to events and appearances throughout Michigan. Super Cherry is proud to be the official mascot of the National Cherry Festival. Look for him at the Open Space and at events throughout the National Cherry Festival.*

This cherry isn't the hero that the festival wants, but it's the one that it deserves. (That bit is my contribution to his tale, and yes, I am a slight fan of Batman.)

Some find it a bit strange that Super Cherry's favorite food is "Fresh Cherries, dried Cherries and anything with Cherries in it," but that's fodder for a whole other book.

The modern National Cherry Festival is a well-oiled machine, rich in history (obviously!) and chock-full of modern charm. It has something for every person, and despite its age, tradition and mission, it is liquid and ever changing. As Traverse City changes and as the wants of cherry fest attendees change, so changes the festival.

Instead of droning on and on about things I was only on the fringe of, I decided to close this final historical chapter out with a few first-person words from a man who was on the frontlines of the festival for almost two decades.

Denny Braun was the 2006 National Cherry Festival president, and he also spent sixteen years on the festival's executive committee. Here, he talks a bit about his time at the helm of the Cherry Festival and his memories of the festival itself:

> *Even as a kid growing up in Traverse City, I remember there were cherry processing plants and storage buildings on the waterfront as well as the Traverse City power plant. As Traverse City's future looked more toward the beauty of the area and the tourists that beauty would attract, all of these* [bay-blocking eyesores] *eventually were removed. The National Cherry Festival was the main ingredient that put TC on the map as a great place to come and live as well as vacation and start a business. Every year, more and more people were introduced to the Traverse City area until tourism became the second largest employer in the area, which has allowed other events and festivals to start and thrive. The National Cherry Festival has created a great opportunity for both business and individuals to live and grow in Traverse City.*

Denny really hits the nail on the head here. Whenever any other festival in the area is mentioned, proposed or talked about, that festival is inevitably compared to the "granddaddy of them all," the National Cherry Festival. Even Traverse City mainstays like the Traverse City Film Festival, the Micro Brew and Music Festival and others began in the National Cherry Festival's shadow. Now, thanks to a community that loves and supports the arts and all manner of entertainment, so many amazing festivals are able to thrive.

But this success hasn't come without struggle. Braun said:

From 1983, when my wife, Jeri, and I started to volunteer, there have been numerous struggles and hurdles. From the loss of our home office on the bay, to whether we were growing the festival the way the community thought was right, to the money struggles making sure our business plan would keep us viable and, of course, local political battles that we tried our best to stay out of. From the late 1980s until the early 2000s, we grew from an organization with a budget of about $250,000 to an annual budget of over $2 million. We had some great leadership from the community members on our board at that time, and it was an exciting time to be part of the festival. We bought a new home on Sixth Street, had to sell and moved to a new home. We produced some of the best large-name concerts in the area with great success, and then the landscape changed, and we lost money for a couple of years and had to change direction again. The executive committee supported the opportunity to help remove the last commercial building on the downtown bay front and the National Cherry Festival was the first to pledge $50,000 towards that project to help make it happen. There are probably many more examples, but the most important is that because of our great community support and our volunteers, both on the boards and all of the volunteers that work our great event, we make it work and we always will.

I spent sixteen years on the executive committee, four years of which as the financial officer. In 2005, I was voted in as president-elect, was then the president in 2006 and served as past president in 2007, my last year on the board. The year I was president, we hired a new executive director for the first time in ten years. The work started in earnest to change the board to a more manageable size. Our board at one time existed of almost one hundred directors, all with a vote. 2007 was the last year of the old board style, and it was decided that we would change to a smaller fifteen-person board with several requirements as who would be members. We also started to work on the relationships between local government and the

Record Eagle. *We also sold our offices on Sixth Street to help us with our financial situation. Those moves began the process of putting us on a path to financial stability and a much better feeling of the direction we needed to go in.*

When you get right down to it, the National Cherry Festival truly is a part of Traverse City's DNA and a true driver of the region's future. According to Braun:

The National Cherry Festival is still, and will continue to be, a driving force to help the growth of the area, bring it notoriety and introduce visitors and businesses alike to what a great region we live in. We also work very hard to support the cherry industry with the information and advertising we generate because of the festival.

The festival is also a point of pride for the community. We have been named in the top ten best festivals in the country for years. We are a family driven event with about 85 percent of our events within the festival free to our visitors. This makes it a challenge to find ways to finance the festival, but one that we are committed to continue.

It has helped the community and region in so many ways, it is hard to place it into words. Both my wife and I were born and raised in Traverse City. Back in the sixties, when we graduated, there was nothing to keep young people here. Nothing going on, very few career opportunities, everyone left to go to college or to find a way to make a living because we were just this small town. Through the years, and with a lot of effort, things started to change, and one of those changes was the National Cherry Festival introducing the rest of the world to what a great place we had to both grow a family and to build a business. What you see here today is a community that is vibrant and fun, filled with all kinds of activity and more, having the ability to carve out a living; all of the pieces are here. Along with the Chamber of Commerce, Traverse City Tourism and other community leaders like the Oleson family and the Beiderman family, all of what you see today is what makes Traverse City what it is. I don't believe the world would have found Traverse City and what it has to offer to the level it has without the National Cherry Festival, a worldwide known destination for family, fun, activities, beauty and a great place live.

Chapter 7
THE QUEEN IN HER OWN WORDS

Sure, there are Ferris wheels, elephant ears, turkey legs, copious amounts of cherries, pies, floats and music galore (and so much more), but when it comes right down to it, none of that will send a shiver of excitement up your spine and put a bigger (or more giddy) grin on your face than shaking hands with that most lovely of ladies bearing the tall, sparkling crown.

Since its inception, the National Cherry Festival has been a most outstanding tool for spreading the wonderful word of cherries to the world. And the person most sought after to do that is the woman who rules over the festival itself. Nowadays, you'll see her much like you would in years gone by. She'll be adorned in a crown, a sash and a smile. Her wit is quick, her knowledge deep and her smile contagious. She is the National Cherry Festival queen, and she truly does command quite a presence.

At its core, the queen program is part scholarship, part ambassadorship. The festival gives her money for college, and she gives voice to the cherry market of the Grand Traverse region.

For many queens during the first few decades of the festival, being National Cherry Queen allowed them to travel outside of the state or to climb on a plane for the first time, something they may have never done had it not been for being queen. The people they met, the places they went and the things that they did may have never happened had they not found the crown. This being queen is truly a life-changing thing!

Do you recall that bit of minutiae a few chapters ago? Well, prepare yourself, detail lovers, because here we go again!

The National Cherry Festival in Traverse City

What follows here is a listing of the queens, from the very first to the current glorious monarch at this writing. Following this, we sit down with the 2003–04 National Cherry Queen, Kelly Plucinski, to hear about what it is to be queen.

1925 – Gertrude Brown
1926 – Charlotte Kearns
1927 – no festival (Remember? Bad crop!)
1928 – Helen Boughy
1929 – Margaret Bachi
1930 – Signe Holmer
1931 – Maxine Weaver
1932 – Carolyn Hazzard
1933 – Morella Oldham
1934 – Anna May York
1935 – Genevieve Pepera
1936 – Ardis Manney
1937 – Eliene Lyon
1938 – Josephine LeFrainer
1939 – Jean Halmond
1940 – Barbara Brown
1941 – Christie Michels
1942 to 1947 – No festivals (Remember? World War II!)
1948 – VonnieVerno
1949 – Anne Maurer
1950 – Joyce English
1951 – Mary Lonn Trapp
1952 – Ruth Madonna Belanger
1953 – Evenl Meloche
1954 – Gail Krahnke
1955 – Sharon Dolan
1956 – Nancy Phillips
1957 – Kay Lahym
1958 – Marcia Wamsley
1959 – Melissa Tornberg
1960 – Murrie Tompkins
1961 – LuEllen Benson

1962 – Geri Schmidt
1963 – Mary Kardes
1964 – Elaine Sanford
1965 – Linda Hale
1966 – Mary Jane Nolan
1967 – Linda Kaye Christie
1968 – Julie Ann Hamilton
1969 – Barbara Ann Beckett
1970 – Paula Ann Maxwell
1971 – Trudy Ann Lindsey
1972 – Trudy Yarnell
1973 – Rebecca Jean Rolsen
1974 – Lois Jean Rider
1975 – Dorinda Murray
1976 – Carol Murray Grishaw
1977 – Patricia Cima
1978 – Ann Alward
1979 – Marlene Polus
1980 – Susan Smith
1981 – Lynn Van Bogelen
1982 – Cheryl Powell
1983 – Angell Dunn
1984 – Kimberlee Broome
1985 – Michele Reitz
1986 – Joy VanderSteen
1987 – Cindy Pleva
1988 – Holly Ann Clark
1989 – Elizabeth Gertz
1990 – Karen Brzeznski
1991 – Mitzie McKay
1992 – Susan Beth Olney
1993 – Ami Lynn Curtiss
1994 – Christina Wills
1995 – Sara Veliquette

1996 – Amy Houdek
1997 – Miranda Kogelman
1998 – Kelli Kaberle
1999 – Erin Sullivan
2000 – Jennifer Brakel
2001 – Kelsey Hewitt
2002 – Ashley Prusick
2003 – Kelly Plucinski
2004 – Maggie Schneider
2005 – Courtney Fountain
2006 – Kaley Schroeder
2007 – Danielle Moss
2008 – Megan Umulis
2009 – Angela Sayler
2010 – Maria LaCross
2011 – Jordan Blaker
2012 – Meg Howard
2013 – Sonya Sayler

Once again, I could drone on and on about what it means to be the queen. But, why would I do that when one of my favorite people on this planet is a cherry queen?

Kelly Plucinski, also known by her ultra-ninja screen name Kelly Kula (for she is living the Hollywood life these days), was crowned queen in 2003. For the year that spanned Cherry Festival 2003 and Cherry Festival 2004, her life was that of glamour, hard work, relationship building and a whirlwind of travel, speaking and appearing. I was able to catch up with her for a moment or two (for her life yet remains quite whirlwind-like) and chat a bit about what it means to be the queen.

"The cherry queen is the key ambassador for both the National Cherry Festival and the Cherry Marketing Institute," explains Kelly. "As with most organizations, a point person is necessary, and having a young, articulate, eager, passionate, crown bearing spokesperson is very helpful. As was the case when I went to Texas, the crown gained me access to many places where others weren't allowed, granting me the ability to talk to people who may never have been accessible. We always called it 'the power of the crown,' but it really wasn't a joke. The crown catches your attention, and when it's followed up by someone who's knowledgeable and positive, it's sure to make waves."

Despite the crown's power and appeal, becoming and being queen is certainly no easy journey. Kelly recalled:

> *Out of the blue, the year before, I decided that I wanted to run for Cherry Queen. Funny as it may sound, I remember eating at KFC with my mom in 2002, and it was then that I asked her what her thoughts were on it. The thought had been floating around in my head for some time, but I was insecure about the decision and needed the opinion and reassurance of my mom. She was instantly behind me and supported me the whole way*

The National Cherry Festival in Traverse City

Queen Kelly begins her reign in style!

through. I liked the idea of being in a position of power in order to do good, and I was excited that my love of public speaking could actually be put to good use. It was literally something that just entered my brain and my brain instinctively knew to hold on to! So, I attended Selection Weekend, went through the process, and ended up being one of the five selected for the Queen's court.

I remember Cherry Festival being an emotional ride that year, and despite wanting it badly enough, I instinctively knew that this year wasn't my year. Regardless, when the results were read at coronation, I was still devastated when I neither won nor was a runner-up. I honestly didn't think that I would run again because it was so emotionally taxing.

So, while attending the Miss Elk Rapids pageant in 2003, I was approached by a few festival members who urged me to run again. Their complete confidence and belief in me made me reevaluate why I wasn't running. I decided then and there that it was a challenge that I wanted to undertake again, and this time, I wanted to do it right. I got the best advice from a former queen: "keep a journal and write positive entries in it every day, i.e. why I would make a great queen, what was special about me, etc." It was difficult for me because we were always taught to be humble, but it was then I realized the line between cockiness and confidence.

Writing these journal entries actually boosted my confidence in something I had little faith in before: simply being happy with being myself. It was that simple strategy that I rode in on when entering the competition for the second year. I was surrounded by amazing, intelligent, passionate women, but this time, I didn't let their positive qualities psych me out. I was able to appreciate their uniqueness while still reminding myself that I was just as valuable. At the end of Selection Weekend, I was again selected to be on the Queen's court.

Kelly said with a smile:

This festival was definitely different. I had an amazing time. I didn't focus on what I didn't have yet, rather on the qualities that I possessed, and that was freeing and allowed me to soak in this amazing opportunity to the fullest. I was 100 percent myself, in all my quirks and attributes, and it wasn't that I didn't care what others thought, but I fearlessly presented myself without worry of being judged.

Granted, when it came to coronation that year, I remember sitting backstage feeling a little nauseous. What if I went out there and lost again? What if being myself wasn't the key to winning this competition? Again, I wanted to win so badly and was worried sick that it may not turn out as I had hoped. I was reassured by a loving festival member that all would be OK.

What happened next is hard to remember clearly. I remember being on stage with the stage lights blaring on our faces, holding hands with the other girls who also wanted to win. They called the first runner-up, my friend Brandi, and I was sincerely excited for her. While they were about to announce the queen, I remember a distinctive calm coming over me. It was as if my nerves completely dissipated and I knew right then that I had won.

"The 2003–04 National Cherry Queen is and always will be... Kelly Plucinski!"

Elation cannot even come close to what I felt. It was a huge validation to me that being yourself can get you exactly where you want to be. The rest of the night is a blur of congratulations and dancing and photographs and interviews. I was so excited for this chapter in my life that when they asked me if I accepted the responsibility of cherry queen, I responded with an overly enthusiastic "Yes, please!" That moment will definitely always be remembered.

Once the crown was placed and the 2003 festival had ended, the real work began for Kelly:

Being cherry queen is like having cherry juice surging through your veins. Promoting the festival and the industry was always on my mind. While in the midst of other summer festivals, I would travel throughout Michigan in order to promote and there was literally an event every single weekend. I looked forward to it as it was the most rewarding job that I have had to that date. During the fall, I was in my senior year of college, but I didn't let that deter me from continuing my promotions; after all, due to my cherry queen scholarship, I would be graduating college debt-free. I was in the theater department and every month I would blanket the staff's mailboxes with cherry-related paraphernalia. I was known throughout the program as the cherry queen and it was a lot of fun dispelling the negative stereotypes that having a crown often entails. My department was great and allowed me to adjust my schedule for events that fell during school time. Even if it wasn't expected of me, I always had an outline of a speech that I would be able to give at every event if anyone had asked me to speak. I love learning so it was a fun challenge adapting my speeches to whichever venue I was attending. I was constantly refreshing myself with cherry facts and keeping up to date with information that was expected from me. I enjoyed it because it fueled my love of being a student.

It's honestly very difficult to narrow down all the awesome things that I experienced during my reign, because every single event literally made my year; each one as significant and important as the last. Some of the highlights were traveling to the Grapevine Festival in Texas and the Rose Bowl in California. Going to Texas was my first flight ever, so that alone was exhilarating. We flew into Texas during a storm, so having to land in Tennessee to get gas because we were running low was definitely a little nerve-wracking. I realized the power of the crown while in Texas because wherever I went, I was treated with such respect and honor that it really allowed me to open doors that may not have previously been opened. Having the crown allowed me to meet all the people I desired in order to spread my passion of the industry and our festival. We shared our trip with a few other festival representatives from other states, and it was a ball getting to know them and their festivals, as well as having a little friendly competition to see who could have the most effective marketing. It was very important to go to that festival as it showed just how important having a queen ambassador can be for a town.

> *The Rose Bowl was mind-blowing, and so much happened, during this trip that it's hard to narrow it down in detail. I do remember standing outside on the balcony of my hotel and realizing that I could definitely call this place home (which I did later that year). Being the National Cherry Queen at the Rose Bowl opened so many new opportunities, and it left me feeling very blessed and humbled. Again, it showed the power of the crown and I felt as if I could do so much good by the people who allowed me access. We were behind the scenes building floats, meeting Jay Leno, and experiencing California, and I knew in my heart I wouldn't have been there if it weren't for being queen.*
>
> *The number one thing that goes through my mind when thinking back on my time as queen is the amazing "family" that I obtained. Every single person who is involved with the festival has touched my life in some way, and the love and outpouring of support was so overwhelming and appreciated. These people still keep in contact with me to this day and it feels so wonderful to have them in my life. Namely, my president, George Wertman, and his wife, Kay, are literally my second family. Traveling throughout the U.S. with them brought us very close and even though my reign has been over for some time, we still keep in contact and celebrate holidays when we can. I was blessed to meet them because I couldn't imagine my life without them.*

For Kelly, being queen wasn't just about cherries or one year of her life. It was, and is, her: who she is today, who she strives to be tomorrow and who she hopes those around her can be as well. This title of queen doesn't leave you when the crown does. She said:

> *Becoming the National Cherry Queen was a huge turning point for me as it solidified my personal confidence in myself. Doing what I do now, acting on a professional level, having self-confidence is crucial to success. If I didn't learn the lesson of "being myself, as is, is enough," I don't think I would be as far along as I am today. As an actor, I get rejected on a daily basis, and if I didn't know how not to take that personally, I would be destroyed as an artist. But through my experience as the National Cherry Queen, I have this confidence in myself that has only gotten stronger and has made me a better individual. Without my reign, my process would have taken a lot longer.*

Before we parted ways, so to speak, I asked her to give us a little tidbit of insider info. She knew exactly what bit needed to be told.

The crown is an eight-inch-tall tiara, all of the eight inches being right on the crown of my head. Like most queens, I had a permanent indent in my head that the crown would just nestle into due to how many events I attended. But before my head got accustomed to wearing the crown, there was often a lot of pain associated with wearing it. I think carrying pain relievers was a necessity for the first part of my reign!

Sort of brings new meaning to "Heavy hangs the head that bears the crown," no?

Chapter 8
THE TOWN THAT CHERRY SELLS

There certainly is much more to being the world's cherry capital than holding a single festival every year. While that single festival is the epitome of joyous cherry celebration, it is, by no means, the only way in which one can experience the cherry here in Traverse City.

For many, the first bit of cherry occurs at touchdown. Many will choose to fly into town for the National Cherry Festival. When their plane touches down, they'll be greeted by Traverse City's Cherry Capital Airport. From there, they can take a Cherry Capital Cab to the heart of downtown or perhaps to the beautiful Cherry Tree Inn.

Either way, once downtown, these intrepid travelers will no doubt notice the Park Place Hotel towering over the streets of Traverse City. Granted, this place doesn't have "cherry" in the name, but it certainly does have it in the soul, what with being so intertwined as part of the history of the festival itself over the years and decades.

From their home base, visitors can spread out throughout downtown. They'll find cherry t-shirts, cherry bumper stickers, cherry art and cherry décor. They find themselves in a sea of tasteful elegance, surrounded by an ocean of awesome kitsch. You can even wake up with an official cup of National Cherry Festival coffee, courtesy of Lansing's Paramount Coffee. According to the company's website, proceeds from the sales of that National Cherry Festival brand coffee go to support the festival, so you can feel good about that cup of joe.

And just to prove that festival really is a liquid brute (in that it changes with the times, while maintaining its utterly awesome roots), while you savor

A grouping of 1955's best and brightest queens.

that Cherry Festival coffee, you can flip through the Cherry Festival app on your smartphone. You can keep up with the festival's social media postings, various announcements, videos, updated events, exclusive contests and more. This thing truly is a festival of the people, willing to go where the people are.

One cherry-centric brand that has endured since 1989 is Paul Sutherland's Cherry Republic. Paul began his business in Glen Arbor by selling 3,500 t-shirts out of the trunk of his car, and more than two decades later he has four successful locations spread across western Michigan. Cherry Republic continues the time-honored tradition of selling cherry-themed merchandise.

Benjamin Twiggs, another Traverse City fixture, has been treating customers to a wide and delectable range of cherry products for nearly half a century. Founded in 1966, Benjamin Twiggs is a proud and perennial sponsor of the Cherry Festival, and the proceeds from the store's sales of Cherry Festival merchandise help to support the event.

A wander into Kilwin's, Doug Murdick's or a score of other sweet arenas will find one in the midst of cherry fudge, ice cream, chocolates and more.

BLESSING OF THE BLOSSOMS

The National Cherry Festival in Traverse City

All manner of cherry desserts adorn shop fronts and store shelves throughout downtown. But what sort of heathen eats dessert without a meal? Aside from the author of this book, of course...

A wander through the National Cherry Festival's main space will offer up all manner of cherry-based delicacies, from burgers to BBQ sauce, hot sauce to bread, salsa to sausage and so much more. The cherry really is an amazing fruit.

The cherry is even good for your overall health. Michigan State University researchers were some of the first to identify powerful anthocyanins in tart cherries, with the potential to inhibit the growth of colon cancer tumors.

According to legendary natural health practitioner Dr. Joseph Mercola, "Cherries, along with many other berries, are a rich source of antioxidants. They help prevent or repair the damage that is done to the body's cells by free radicals. This means that antioxidants replace free radicals in your body before they can cause any damage."

According to many sources within the healthcare community, cherries (mostly in the raw state, but oftentimes prepared as well, as long as mountains of sugar are not added to the recipe) help the body fight disease, help in pain relief, help the body fight stress and much more.

This fruit certainly is worthy of celebration! And what would be a better way to celebrate this fruit than by creating amazing brews around it from which to sup after a hearty (and heartfelt) toast?

"The Cherry Pie Whole came about during a conversation at lunch with Denise and Mike from Grand Traverse Pie Company," recalls Right Brain Brewery founder and owner Russell Springsteen. "The Chamber of Commerce had arranged for us to speak at the U of M entrepreneurial speakers forum. We were in the process of developing the Pig Porter. We needed to figure out how to get the fat out. Well, I give credit to Denise because she said we should brew a pie beer. A great business relationship was formed."

"Cherry Pie Whole is classified as an amber ale," explains Right Brain's head brewer Nick Panchame. "It is made with forty cherry crumble pies from Grand Traverse Pie Company. Half are added to the barrel pre-fermentation. Half are added to the fermenter and aged for around ten days. The beer is then chilled for a period of time to solidify any remaining oils from the crust. The whole process takes about two to three weeks. On our menu it is described as being an amber ale having a smooth and full mouth feel, strong cherry aroma, and showcases notes of fruit, vanilla and butter."

Made with more than forty whole cherry pies, this beer is perfection on a summer's afternoon.

The National Cherry Festival in Traverse City

"The first glass of any of our beers almost always goes to either our owner Russell or our brewers," explains Right Brain's Leif Kolt. "To ensure the highest quality products, we're constantly tasting our beers all the way down the production line, so that by the time they go on tap anywhere, the 'first glass' is long gone. Plus, when you've been working on something for several weeks in a row, and paying such close attention to it, you become pretty attached. Being one of the first people to sample the fruits of your labor is extremely rewarding. Aside from that, we try our hardest to make sure that every beer that comes out of the tap tastes just as good as the first, so in that way, everyone gets the first pint."

For businesses like Right Brain, the National Cherry Festival is an opportunity to showcase the unique bits and pieces that make Traverse City such an outstanding place to be. But when you're Right Brain (or any of the other outstanding breweries in the area), you've got an added bonus that many other businesses with cherry-themed products simply do not have: beer.

"When people visit Traverse City, they're all looking for something fun to do that represents our region," says Leif. "For us, that means cherry-themed food, wine and beer. People want to see what Traverse City is about, so all the businesses pull out the big guns. At Right Brain, that means we make beer with cherry pies. Also, because of the traffic, it seems like lots of Traverse City locals try and hang out away from the chaos of downtown, and since our brewery is centrally located but still outside of the epicenter of downtown, many of these people will make us their hangout for the week."

Now, I am fully aware that there are those among you who prefer something other than beer, and while I do not understand you, I empathize and offer you a hearty "No worries!"

If the visitor to Traverse City happens to be a fan of wine, then they are in luck! Cherry wine, or even a cherry wine slushy, can be found everywhere, as can all of the more traditional and favored brands of Michigan wine.

But if that visitor seeks a true treat, they need to seek out Northern Natural Cider House in downtown Traverse City.

"We are planning for a Cherry Gala at the Cider House this year," says Northern Natural's Jen Mackey while discussing plans for Cherry Fest 2014.

And what will that gala offer the intrepid cherry lover? Jen explains:

> *We have a bit of something for everyone. We dedicate five taps for cherry hard cider blends. We also feature a small "corktail" menu consisting of mixers from our cherry wines and hard ciders, as well as highlighting food specials that incorporate cherries. Our five taps include the Traffic Jam (a barrel-aged—whiskey barrel from GT Distillery—cherry cider), our cherry-apple hard cider (a natural balance of tart and sweet), the Cherry Bomb (cherries and berries), our cherry lemongrass (lemon aroma, ripe cherry, slight ginger) and our cherry-ginger (ginger and cinnamon aroma, tart and spicy, yet semi sweet). All are cherry must-haves for the season!*
>
> *We also offer a Cherry Mojito Corktail, some awesome cherry salsa and cherry hummus, a fun cherry chicken pizza and more.*
>
> *Northern Michigan is a great growing area for cherries. Tasty cherries come out of our loamy soil and hearty climate. We have been making our own certified organic cherry concentrate for years, and we utilize our local family farms for our organic cherries.*

While cherries are certainly tasty, versatile bits of food, they aren't always sweet and innocent.

"Our community is very athletic-minded," says Traverse City Roller Derby (TCRD) founder Lori Piggot. "We love and support the Red Wings and various hockey leagues, Beach Bums, Blues Rugby, TC Wolves, along with many other adult sports teams, as well as plenty of high school and

The National Cherry Festival in Traverse City

TCRD ace Mace Hindu makes the leap over one of her TCRD family members, while Kamikaze Kuch lines up for his turn.

middle school teams. What better place to start a roller derby league than a town that embraces sports?"

So with that in mind, Lori and her core crew set out to get roller derby rolling. She did so with the Traverse City Toxic Cherries and then later with the league's b-team, the Traverse City Cherry Bombs.

Lori explained:

> *We held a public naming contest via e-mail and drop boxes at local businesses. Choosing a name that referenced our local ties was important in order to garner as much local support as possible. Traverse City is well known for a variety of attractions and reasons, and we had hundreds of great entries, so it was difficult to decide. When our committee met to go through all of the entries, the cherry theme kept surfacing as the frontrunner. Toxic Cherries was the name with the most votes by our membership, because it referenced our local heritage while giving us an edge to be recognized.*
>
> *One of the reasons I love Traverse City so much is that anyone can be here and feel welcome, there is a place for everyone. Our community is a warm group of people who want to see others succeed, we wish for the best for anyone willing to put forth the effort. We also like variety. We want the strong family traditions that give us what is familiar and comforting.*

We also want to see and experience new things. It makes perfect sense that the Cherry Festival and roller derby work so well in our town. And like most other non-profit organizations, we both promote volunteerism, local businesses and family fun. And who in TC can't get behind those kinds of efforts?

For so many in the region, Traverse City in the summer and cherries go hand in hand. And anyone who has ever been a part of a Traverse City summer is certainly hooked for life, even if that "anyone" is a hard-as-nails derby girl.

"Summer in Traverse City is magical," says Lori. "The beaches, local shops, people, festivals and all the surrounding areas help make this the home in which I want to live and raise my family. The National Cherry Festival is definitely an integral part of that equation. It's been our most well-known attraction for generations; it's one of the things that help put Traverse City on the map as a beautiful place to vacation and to live. I can't imagine a Traverse City without a Cherry Festival. "

Chapter 9
THE STORIES

There is certainly a lot to be said for historical accuracy, rampant record keeping, obsessive list making and a general love for all things historical. There's nothing quite like a box full of receipts, photographs, ledgers and newspaper articles for a historical buff. But this box doesn't necessarily bring an event to life. This box gives you the cold, hard facts. While those certainly are valuable, they aren't the stuff of life within the event itself.

1955 queen candidates relax before the parade.

Within these stories, you'll find wistful memories, happy experiences, an ideal evening or a perfect afternoon. Within these stories, you will find the tale and the soul of the National Cherry Festival.

LACHLAN BROCKMILLER, AGE ELEVEN

A cool kid went to the Cherry Festival carnival and went into the house of mirrors. Inside he crashed into the glass mirrors over and over because the glass was crystal clear and it looked like a passageway. He didn't stop trying to get through. Finally, he saw a staircase but it was a reflection in the crystal clear mirror. He found the real staircase and walked up. He slid down the slide and finally got out. It was awesome!

IVY WALKER, AGE ELEVEN

Almost every year we go to the Open Space to make Cherry pies. You put on an apron and a little hat. They give you a little tin pie pan. You get a little ball of dough and you roll it out with the rolling pin. Then you press the dough inside the tin and right around the edges. They give you all of the ingredients, like a cup of Cherries, some sugar, and flour. After the pie pan is filled with all of the ingredients, they give you another piece of dough to roll out. You put that over all of the ingredients and pinch it around the edges so it doesn't come off while baking. You get a sticky note to write your first and last name on and stick it to the side of the pan. Then, you give it to the baking people and they put it in the oven. You leave and come back in an hour. The pies are done and you can eat them then. And it's all free at the Cherry Festival!

CAMERON, AGE SIX

I am going to be Prince of the Cherry Festival and I get to ride the float! It's going to be awesome!

Festival princesses and princes wait patiently at Thirlby Field.

LUKE

I love the roller coaster! The drop goes straight down on the track. This is the order: straight, up, straight, drop, and then straight again!

CHLOE TAYLOR, AGE SEVEN

I am the Princess for Cherry Fest this year. I get to ride on the float and I get to build the float too! I will have a lot of fun and I get to wear a very pretty dress. I will have a special meeting with the people at the office. I will have so much fun! I can't wait until it is Summer!

JACOB ALLEN TRICK, AGE SEVEN

You're writing a Cherry Fest book? Cam's the Prince and Chloe is the Princess!

SPENCER STALLMAN, AGE SEVEN

I went to the Cherry Festival! I went on the Egyptian boat and swung up and down!

LUCY BONGIORNO, AGE SIX

The Cherry Festival has a lot of floats! All of the first graders ride the float. Every year, there is a Prince and a Princess. They sit on the front of the float. There is a different theme at each of the schools. They pass out candy and toys!

MALLORY RHEM, AGE SEVEN

The Cherry Festival has rides and lots of floats. On every float it has a Prince and a Princess. I like the Cherry Festival because you get to watch the floats. And, if you go to the rides, it has a thing that you go slow at first and then you go super fast. That ride is my favorite. It also has real fast other rides.

AIDEN FAIRBANK, AGE SEVEN

I went on Area 51. There's a man that talks into a microphone that makes his voice scary. You have no belt and you're being sucked to the wall so tight you can't really move. It's like you're glued to the wall.

ANNIE GOLDKUHLE, AGE SEVEN

Elephant ears are so big! They taste good. They look like big elephant ears but they're just food. They put them on a plate. You have to use two hands to eat them. I forget what they taste like, but they were good!

IALI RODENROTH, AGE SEVEN

In 2011 my brother Lucas was Prince for Cherry Festival. The theme of the float was New York. I got to ride on the float. It was so soso fun! I want to do it again!

MARIXZA GOMEZ, AGE SEVEN

Last Cherry Festival I rode the swings. The swings start off slow, then they get fast. When the swings get slow again, the ride is over and a little girl got off. When she got off, she threw up. And everyone felt bad for her. Even I did! Then everyone went home.

WESLEY NICULA, AGE SEVEN

I was sitting with my grandma and grandpa and my grandma said a color to a clown that stopped by us. The clown opened a suitcase and then closed it. We had to guess the right color of the pen, but we didn't pick the right color. Well, grandma didn't pick the right color. She should have picked pink.

ELYSE HEFFNER, AGE SEVEN

At the Cherry Festival, I got to ride in a police car because my dad is a police officer. We get to lead the whole parade! I love it! After, we get to go to Moomer's and we get to see the cows and sometimes we get to go home and play in the sprinklers. And, always, our friends come over for a week! I love the Cherry Festival!

ZACHARY CHAUSSEE, AGE SEVEN

At the Cherry Festival there is a big flower pot. It has one or two cherries and the words "Cherry Festival" in it. The flowers get planted in the Spring.

KD CONWAY, AGE SIX

At the Cherry Festival I saw some of my friends. Katlin and I went on the drop. We all had fun.

CARTER BANTON, AGE SEVEN

One day, I went on the Ferris wheel with my mom and little brother. I felt great! I was having a great time. When I was up there, I saw a bird.

MITCHELL MILLARD, AGE SIX

You should see the hot dog! It is a big, giant dog!

JAMESON NICULA, AGE TEN

I really like riding on the floats! I ride with the Roller Derby girls because my mom is a Roller Derby girl. They're a lot more fun than some people. I really like being in the parade, it's a fun view watching the people watching you. Last year, I got to ride my friend's scooter in the parade, that was awesome!

KAREN COUTURIER

My siblings and I were raised on the street where the parade would line up each year. This was in the 700 block of State Street, in fact, they still line up here. Back in the '50s, the lineup was only about two blocks long, and the F&M Park was not cleaned up for use. We would ride on the floats in our younger days, but before that we would ride our bikes up and down the street looking at all of the floats and the people that would be on them. Our father would work on floats each year at the old fair grounds. He spent many an hour at night and on the weekends there. My mother was always excited when the floats started to line up. This day also brought relatives from down state to our house. Mom would feed them and they had a good place to park in the alley. Nowadays, I enjoy walking down the streets as they line up. I don't know many people anymore, but it sure does bring back memories!

MAI IA VANG, AGE TWENTY-NINE

When I think of Traverse City, I can't imagine it without the Cherry Festival. I still remember going for the first time with my siblings nineteen years ago. I can smell the cinnamon from the elephant ears, the smoky jumbo turkey legs and vinegar from Gibby's fries. I love hearing kids laugh and adults screaming at the top of their lungs on rides. The best part about the Cherry Festival is that we have people from all over the country come and celebrate it. It's one of my favorite times of the year because I get to see my entire family. There's nothing like taking my nieces and nephews to the Cherry Festival and watching them smile and laugh the way I did as a kid.

CHRIS CAROL, AGE THIRTY-ONE

For many, summer is baseball and hot dogs. Summer is sun and beaches; swimming, camping, cooking on the grill—generally feeling slightly scorched.

For me, it is not very different—those things still resonate with my notion of summer—but truth be told: little is as synonymous with "summer" as "Cherry Fest."

The National Cherry Festival in Traverse City

My dad was a GM guy; he started with the AC-Delco plant in Flint, Michigan, and later went elsewhere, always staying in the automotive industry. Growing up, all that meant little to me—except that each summer he had two full weeks off. So, each summer, sometime around the end of June and the beginning of July, my mom, dad, sister and I would pack up into a cramped, cream-colored 1980 Chevy Chevette and make the journey north to Beulah, where my great-grandfather lived. The next two weeks would be spent on the beach of Crystal Lake, or at the putt-putt course across the street, or the library in Benzie, at the movie theater in Frankfort...

Until Cherry Fest week.

Cherry Fest's arrival was preceded, to a degree, by the arrival of each of my respective aunts and uncles. The more family that cramped into my great grandfather's two-bedroom cottage (by this point, I was sleeping on a cot, sharing the laundry/mud room with my sister), the sooner it was that we'd all head over to Traverse City for the Cherry Fest.

Each of us had our own favorite Cherry Fest things.

I remember my Aunt Denise and Uncle Dave were happy to hear some band I can no longer recall play.

I remember my mom and dad tell me stories about how they got sick on the tilt-a-whirl when they were in high school together and how they'd never ride that ride again.

I remember my grandpa being generally upset about the traffic and parking situations.

I remember I just took things in. Too young at the time to grasp tradition. Too naïve to know that every Cherry Fest (like every moment) is different and cannot be distilled into so many words.

Too foolish to think the sun couldn't hurt me; that the shade of the Cherry Fest booths would protect my nose and the back of my neck. But I'm stilling feeling its effects—whether from the sun or the summer or Cherry Fest in general—who's to say?

LISA KELLY, AGE THIRTY-TWO

I have many memories of the Cherry Festival. I grew up in Traverse City and have been going to the parade since I was little and long before I probably even remember. Every year, my family goes down to the big parade, the Cherry Royale. Someone goes down early Saturday morning and puts folding chairs out in a good and shady spot where we can watch the parade and not get fried. All of my kids have been to a parade when they were a baby. For their first, my now ten-year-old was three months old, my now seven-year-old was seven months old, and my now two-year-old was six months old. I have memories from just over ten years of the Cherry Festival Parade with my kids. My parents have always been there, and my grandparents have always been there, and I have pictures of multiple generations of my family enjoying the parade. I don't know if I'll remember what was always in the parade, but I will remember our traditions of setting up our chairs and packing lunch and just being with each other on that hot summer day.

KATE SHAPKAROFF, AGE THIRTY-FIVE

I've lived here for just over eight years, and prior to that, I had never heard of the National Cherry Festival. My introduction to the festival was that pretty much all the locals think it's a huge inconvenience with the influx of tourists it brings. After eight Cherry Festivals, I can tell you that I agree with part of that sentiment. The first sights of the massive tents going up at the Open Space are met with a combination of anxiety and excitement. The anxiety is due to the hordes of people that the festival brings in and how our small city is gridlocked with traffic from cars, people, strollers, etc. While most people would call Memorial Day Weekend the start of summer, it's the Cherry Festival that reminds us that we will be wall-to-wall tourists until Labor Day—roughly eight weeks straight.

The excitement is that, love it or hate it, the National Cherry Festival is the calling card for our great city. I also really like cherries, but I don't over indulge in cherry-themed merchandise because that's kind of like wearing the t-shirt of the band you're going to see. There is one thing that most of us locals can agree on: we all end up at the beer tent at least once throughout the festival.

ALISON NEIHARDT

I have memories during Cherry Fest of going downtown in junior high and high school. We would ride our bikes all over town! We would go to the carnival and play games and ride on rides together. We would then go to the open space and, of course, get food. I remember the Keystone Cops locking people up at the Cherry Land Mall. I also remember going to the parades. I would walk downtown with my cousins and we would watch all the floats. This was early to mid-'90s. It was just part of summer in TC!

DENNY BRAUN

After spending thirty-one years as a volunteer with the festival, there are so many memories and moments. Of course, the years I spent on the executive committee were great, as well as being the director of Ambassadors before that. Being president in 2006 was probably the best, being able to include my wife, Jeri, and my daughters, Gina and Devon, and our grandkids riding down Front Street in the grand royal parade, and being able to enjoy that year with all the volunteers and the community. One of my favorite memories was, the year after being president, running operations in the open space. It was a great time and it renewed the fun of being in on the planning and reaffirmed the idea of just how hard our volunteers really work and what a great job they do. Going to IFEA and being one of the volunteers representing the National Cherry Festival was great as well. This was such a great opportunity to learn from festivals and events from all over the country and the world. Many of our events and programs came from going to these yearly gatherings.

KRISTOPHER ZINTH, AGE THIRTY-THREE

I've only experienced a few Cherry Festivals, but one that definitely stands out is the one in which I participated as a member of my school's marching band. We stayed at Central Grade School, that's where we spent the night, sort of camping out style. One, or some, we never found out, of the girls scratched up all of the mirrors in the girls' bathroom. Our band director got so mad at us. He called us all together and went on and on, just yelling and really flipping out. Then he just stopped talking to us. He didn't talk to us at all. The next day, he marched the entire parade route with us in his pajamas. I really think he might have snapped…

MITCH

My dad is pretty hardcore. I remember, as a kid, giving him a beer and a cigarette when he finished the big race while all of the other racers had water.

JEREMY JENNETT, AGE THIRTY-ONE

The greatest experience I had at the Cherry Festival was in first grade. My parents had signed up to help with the school's Cherry Festival prince and princess float. But they never expected to have their own prince! I, Jeremy Jennett, proudly served as a Cherry Festival prince in 1989 for Elk Rapids schools. Everything from bubble gum bubble blowing contests to being on stage with Deputy Dan [an old TV host of a local show] where I misspoke and said I was from Kalkaska Schools. Jenny, the princess, politely corrected me. The most fun I have had in all my years of attending that festival is still the sand castle building contest. Way more fun than the parades, with the Blue Angels in a close second.

JANET KING, AGE FIFTY-FIVE

I'm a lifetime volunteer for the Cherry Festival. My family and I volunteer for the special kids day, as I am also handicapped. This day is always a very special day for these kids and the volunteers. I volunteer at the softball event every year. It doesn't matter if you're in a wheelchair or whatever, it makes no difference what your needs are, you can play softball and participate in all of the activities that we have. It's really great for all of the kids to get involved who have special needs. We have something for everyone. My family comes in from Chicago and Ohio every year, and we always sign up for this because it's so special to us. These kids face hurdles and stigma everyday. This day at the Cherry Festival lets them forget that for a moment and just have fun.

BEVERLY AND GEORGE CRISMAN, AGE SEVENTY-SIX AND EIGHTY-THREE

Bev and I go back to the early '70s. We hardly ever missed a Cherry Festival. At that time, I had a '67 Mustang convertible. Just like new, cherry! Beverly had a '65 Mustang convertible as well. For years, we had the cherry queen on the back of my car during the big parade. We were able to meet Willard Scott and get a picture with him one year. It's always been a great time.

Beverly's mustang is still in Traverse City, actually. Mr. Jonkhoff, the funeral director who owns Perry Hannah's home, has spent quite a bit of time and effort bringing that car back to perfection.

We've pretty much volunteered everywhere at the festival. In the last couple of years, we've been at the beverage tent. Along with that, I'm a Korean War veteran, so that means I get to march in the parade, although I think we're getting too old to march, so they have us up in a truck now, and the jeeps, riding along. When I'm marching, I just can't believe the crowds. It's huge! And this year is really going to be something because the Blue Angels are back.

PATRICIA ROSS (KROUPA), AGE SEVENTY-FIVE

I've lived in Traverse City almost all of my seventy-five years. My dad, Perry, and mother had a big cherry farm out on Old Mission Peninsula. My family have always been in cherries. My entire family, uncles, aunts, everyone has always had cherries. My dad owned Kroupa Incorporated as well, a cherry sorting factory on the Peninsula.

While cherries have always been in the family, my cousins, David and Janet Kroupa, are getting into wine now. It's funny, because my dad, a few years before he died, said "I think we'll move from cherries a bit more into wine." And he couldn't have been more right!

The Cherry Festival has always been really nice. I remember years ago, they used to have a certain night where they'd have tractors from the various farms and all that on parade. It really started as a nice partnership between the farmers and their farms and the festival.

I've been going to the National Cherry Festival ever since I was a little girl. I'd go there and go there and go there! I really liked the Mummer's Parade, but they took that away. But, as the years go on, you have to cater to different people's tastes. I was in the Cherry Pit Spitting Contest quite a few times.

I never won anything, but I sure had fun. I also liked to ride the rides, of course. I liked the tilt-a-whirl a lot. I have some very nice memories of the Cherry Festival.

I definitely plan on going down this year. It's kind of hard now with my walker, but people usually get out of my way because they don't want to get run over.

I really like going down to the carnival still. You see a lot of people from years ago that you knew and don't get to see that much. I love it. You go down and meet your neighbors and you talk and visit. It's so nice to go down and enjoy it.

SUE KELLY

Remember, you have chair duty. Not again! It only happens once a year, but the 4:00 a.m. time comes too early for a Saturday, and maybe this year we'll just take our chances.

But it's the family tradition and part of the community spirit for these past twenty-five years of attending the National Cherry Festival Grand Parade in our beautiful Traverse City. Chair duty goes to the person who sets up all the folding chairs the morning of the parade to guarantee primo viewing among the mobs of people downtown on Front Street. The ordinance says no chairs the night before, so how can there be chairs already at 4:00 a.m.?

The count is taken, and more chairs are needed to seat great-grandparents, grandparents, sons, daughter, son-in-law, daughter-in-law and grandchildren. Looks like two rows this year. Will we get the sweet spot near the band judges where the marching bands always play their best? Several years of baking in the sun have taught us to sit on the shady side of the street for the three-hour spectacle to stay cool and avoid sunburns.

Once the chairs have been placed, the person on chair duty can crawl back into bed for a few more hours of *zzzzzzz*'s. Then it's lunches and drinks in the cooler, hats, and sunglasses and we're off. We make our way through the crowds, glad to have assigned seating and not leaving it to chance. It's the perfect spot, and the chair duty person has executed his job with honor. Everyone smiles, waves American flags just passed out, and sits back to enjoy the parade. Chair duty success again this year, but maybe next year the torch, or rather the chairs, will be passed on to the son-in-law!

YOUR HUMBLE AUTHOR (AND THE SON-IN-LAW REFERENCED IN THE PRECEDING TALE), AGE THIRTY-TWO

I have spent my lifetime on the fringes of the festival. For more than a decade, aside from two years living in Guatemala, I lived in and around Traverse City, always anticipating, enjoying and diving headlong into the festivities. So many memories of this glorious affair fill my mind. But, I admit, I would be remiss if I did not continue the thoughts of my dear mother-in-law and write a bit about the chair placing experience.

My first exposure to this, I'll admit, I was a begrudging participant. I'm a nice guy, so I'm willing to help out. But when I was told that 5:00 a.m. may even be too late to get a good space downtown, I was somewhat less than enthusiastic about the whole affair. I looked to the day ahead after placing the chairs. It was full of parade prep and lining up with the floats. As my amazing wife is a member of the Traverse City Roller Derby league, we take part in both the kid's parade and the "big" parade alongside all of the other TCRD folk. Waking at 4:00 a.m. never sounds like fun when one has all of that to look forward to in the day to come.

But then I did it, and I discovered a side to the National Cherry Festival that I had never known.

As I rode into downtown on my bike, a literal mountain of chairs bungee corded into the kids' cart behind me, I was struck by the feelings of the festival.

It seems strange to say it, but at this early hour, when the trappings and pomp and circumstance of the festival are all still resting, awaiting the crowds, the on-switch flipping, the life force that only a crowd of thousands can provide—there, before me and surrounding me, was the National Cherry Festival of old.

I pulled up to the perfect spot, on the shaded side of the street, near a tree, and began my unloading. The air was crisp and clean, a slight refreshing chill, but hints of the heat to come unmistakable in that chill and humidity.

I paused for a moment and glanced about me and took in what I saw. There were quiet storefronts; banners flapping lazily in the breeze; American flags, freshly put out to greet the sun; going through their morning stretches, a small yoga group was facing east, light on their tranquil faces; and a grandfather was placing a tiny folding chair near to his as his small grandson tried his very best to sit in that chair before the work of unfolding was even done. The morning light was deep yellow, and the breeze carried with it the smell of sand and sunscreen.

A police car rolled along Front Street. The officer waved and smiled a knowing smile at me. He then pointed to a collection of chairs not far from mine and shook his head, still smiling. I laughed and gave him an understanding thumbs-up, as I immediately knew that he was pointing out his own morning mission, no doubt handed down by his parents-in-law.

There were a few red-shirted volunteers wandering with their own chairs and much more than a few very tired-looking young men and women, recruited for their relative youth, I'm sure. But anytime any form of eye contact was made, there was kindness, a smile, a nod and perhaps even a bit of cross-street conversation.

As I placed the last chair, I suddenly was able to identify this feeling that had enveloped me since the beginning of my ride through downtown Traverse City. This was the soul of the festival.

Yes, there is a grand amount of celebrating, a huge amount of hustle and bustle and a near abandonment of the normal pedestrian laws in the city. There is action, laughter, technology, organization, music, food and so much more. But all of that? It wouldn't come until later.

Right now, there was only community, a neighborhood vibe, a child-like anticipation for a time-honored event that was soon to march down Main Street.

There was a father and son enjoying a quiet moment testing out all of the chairs, and there was conversation amongst neighbors and new friends. There was calm and comfort, and there was perfection, right here, in front of these chairs that I had just placed.

In this moment, I could see the fabric of Traverse City laid out before me. Its volunteers, its civil servants, its community members, its businesses, its summer, and, most of all, its festival.

Needless to say, I stopped and sat for a while that morning. And have done the same ever since.

Chapter 10
GET THEE TO THE FESTIVAL!

Lori Hall Steele wrote a book entitled *Sweet and Snappy Cherry Drinks*. The title is exactly what the book is: a plethora of yummy cherry concoctions. But the introduction perfectly sums up the cherry, the National Cherry Festival and the region from which it hails. She writes, "Real cherry isn't sweet like [grocery store juices]. Real cherry tangs in your mouth. It hits with a slight sweetness and something close to sass. Though it rarely overpowers, it has definite presence—its very own cherry mojo."

Truer words on this amazing fruit and the celebration that it has spawned have never been spoken.

Who knows what the future of this festival holds? Perhaps it will grow into a summer-long celebration. Perhaps it will pick up roots and travel the state and the nation. Perhaps it will become more compact or grow to encompass an entire cherry-growing region.

One thing is certain, however. It is here to stay. No one man, woman or movement holds enough sway to change that fact. As the National Cherry Festival's executive director often says, this festival truly is part of the fabric of Traverse City. It is as much a part of the city's identity and consciousness as are the beaches and the water. One simply cannot part the one from the other without completely changing the identity of everything.

And so, as we end this little Cherry Festival journey, I sincerely hope that you are of the mind to give the fest a go. If you've never been, make that journey. Whether you live one block away or one continent, you will meet

The National Cherry Festival in Traverse City

people who have traveled farther than you for generations and who could not fathom a summer without the Cherry Festival.

If you haven't been in a while, get going! This festival is full of fun and fancy for everyone, no matter the age. From entertainment to food, camaraderie and more, the National Cherry Festival showcases all that Traverse City has to offer, and each year that showcasing grows.

And should you find yourself among the midway, the concert stage, the vendors' tents or more, do not neglect the rest of this fine region. This festival really is, as stated before, a celebration of the Grand Traverse community. And, as such, the entire community gets in on the fun. From the downtown shops, to the neighborhood stores, to the outlying markets, everyone has a bit of festival fever for that one week in July.

But were you to find yourself in this lovely hamlet of ours at a time when the fencing has been rolled up, the tents packed away, the tour buses gone, the Ferris wheel shuttled off to some other burg and the turkey legs in frozen storage, do not fear. The spirit of this festival is alive and well throughout the year here in Traverse City. It is in every neighborhood, every shop front, and every friendly smile. The cherry reigns supreme all year long, and the soul of our festival walks these streets whether it be July or the dead of winter.

This National Cherry Festival has begot unto us (bible again) some grand affairs. Without its model, its molding, its leadership and its example, who knows where our other much-loved festivals would be? Would the Traverse City Film Festival be the awesome spectacle of film that it is? Would the wine, food and beer festivals be as delicious, decadent and divine as they now are? Would Traverse City be the city that it is now if there were no National Cherry Festival? Who can say? One thing is for sure. We here in Traverse City, and many of you around the nation and world, certainly are happy that we'll never have to find out the answer to that question. Our community and its festival live on. This perfect slice of Americana, set in the midst of our modern summer, our modern world, is the ideal bit of escapism, exactly what the doctor ordered, as they say.

This National Cherry Festival really is the bee's knees, guys!

Lastly, should you make it to the fest and you happen to see a man with a shaved head and a glorious beard walking alongside a wife who is *much* too beautiful to be in his league and children *much* too adorable to be his own, stop me and say hello!

I'll see you at National Cherry Festival 2014. And every one thereafter. Cherry on!

INDEX

A

ABC 67
A Cherry's Tale 72
Acme 59
Adams, Sarah 70
Alcatraz 37
Alward, Ann 80
American Agricultural Marketing
    Association 63
American Legion Hall 36
Anderson, Keith 70
Anheuser-Busch 35
Antrim County Review 69
Argus Press 52, 67, 70, 71
Arnold Amusements 60, 61, 73
Arnold, Ivan 61
Astoria 28, 29
Atlantic Monthly 14
Aunt Jemima 36

B

Bachi, Margaret 80
Baic, Vojin 44
Bancroft, Edgar 28
Banton, Carter 104
Basch, Don 44
Bayside Festival Stage 58
Beach Bums 70, 95
Beatles, the 37
Becker, Andrea 71
Beckett, Barbara Ann 47, 80
Beiderman 78
Belanger, Ruth Madonna 80
Bensley, Loren 53
Benson, LuEllen 80
Bermuda triangle 69
Better Homes and Gardens 43
Black, Clint 65
Blaker, Jordan 81
Blessing of the Blossoms ceremony 15
Blessing of the Blossoms Festival 20
Blue Angels 57, 69, 70, 109, 110
Blues Rugby 95

INDEX

Boardman, Harry 13
Boccia, Roslyn 42
Bogelen, Lynn Van 80
Bongiorno, Lucy 102
Boone, Debby 58
Boone, Pat 58
Boughey, FP 17
Boughy, Helen 53, 80
Box, Bill 57
Brakel, Jennifer 81
Braun, Denny 9, 76, 108
Brewery Ferment 51
Brockmiller, Lachlan 100
Broome, Kimberlee 80
Brown, Barbara 29, 80
Brown, Gertrude 20, 80
Brown, Prentiss M. 29
Brzeznski, Karen 80
Bulmann, Mitchell August 69
Bush, George 61
Buteyn, Maddie 9

C

California (battleship) 29
Carol, Chris 105
CBS This Morning 67
Center Road 21
chamber of commerce 78
Chapman, William 21
Charlevoix 48, 62, 90
Chaussee, Zachary 104
Chef Pierre 62
Cherry Capital 7, 62, 68, 89
Cherry Capital Airport 62, 68, 89
Cherry Capital Cab 89
Cherry County Playhouse 44, 51
Cherry Dollars 65
Cherry Fest 21, 59, 67, 76, 95, 101, 102, 105, 106, 107
Cherry Festival 8, 9, 11, 20, 26, 30, 33, 37, 48, 52, 57, 59, 60, 62, 63, 67, 69, 70, 71, 73, 76, 77, 81, 83, 90, 97, 100, 102, 103, 104, 105, 106, 107, 109, 110, 111, 115, 116

Cherry Home Canning Company 15
Cherry Industry Day 71
Cherryland Band Classic 49
Cherry Marketing Institute 81
Cherry Pie Whole 92
Cherry Players 44
Cherry Republic 90
Cherry Roubaix 44
Cherry Royale 41, 59, 60, 67, 106
Cherry Royale Parade 59
Cherry Tree Inn 89
Chicago 23
Chicago Mayor Daley 47
Chilean ambassador 29
China Beach USO 47
Chippewa Wranglers Riding Club 43
Christian, Spencer 65, 67
Christie, Linda Kaye 42, 80
Cima, Patricia 80
City Police Department 51
City Recreational Activities 51
Clark, Holly Ann 80
Clinch Park 33
Coast Guard 26, 27, 39, 68, 69
Cochlin, Demas 21
Cold War 43
"Come Live With Me" 51
Comstock, William A. 24, 26
Con Foster Museum 43
Conway, K.D. 104
Couturier, Karen 105
Crisman, Beverly and George 110
Crough, Bryan 67
Curtiss, Ami Lynn 80
Curwood Festival 70
Curwood Festival Queen 70

D

Da Nang 47, 48
Davy Crockett 48
Department of Labor 39
Detroit 48
Detroit Free Press 41, 42
Dinsmore, Dan 9

Index

Dolan, Sharon 80
Doug Murdick's 90
Downtown Traverse City Association 67
Dunn, Angell 80

E

Ebsen, Buddy 48
Edmondson, Harold 68
Eikhoff, Edwin E. 17
Elks Club 71
Ellington, Duke 48
El Tropicano Motor Hotel 50
Engel, Albert 29
Engler, John 65
English, Joyce 33, 80
Escanaba (cutter) 27
Estes, Michael 72

F

Fairbank, Aiden 102
Farkas, Eugene 48
Fat Albert 57
Festival of States 50
Figy, Charles 33
Ford, Gerald 54
Ford, Henry 20
Ford, President and Mrs. 54
Fountain, Courtney 81
French Patrouille de France 57
Friedrich, A.V. 21

G

Gaylord 70
General Motors 37
Gertz, Elizabeth 65, 80
Gibby's 73
Gill, Vince 65
Ginoux, Lucien Pierre 51
Glen Arbor 90
Goldkuhle, Annie 103
Gomez, Marixza 103
Good Morning America 65, 67
Governor's Ball 24, 26
Graceland Fruit 74, 76

Grand Floral Parade 39, 41, 44
grand parade 35, 48, 51, 54, 111
Grand Rapids 70
Grand Traverse 7, 13, 14, 15, 20, 26, 37, 39, 43, 49, 53, 57, 66, 73, 79, 116, 125
Grand Traverse Hilton 59
Grand Traverse Packaging Company 15
Grand Traverse Pie Company 92
Grand Traverse Woolens 43
Grand Traverse Zoological Society 65
Gray, M.E. 44
Great Lakes Triangle 69
Green, Carole, "Miss Greilickville" 44
Grishaw, Carol Murray 80

H

Halmond, Jean 80
Hamilton, Julie Ann 44, 80
Hannah and Lay Company 13
Hannah, Perry 13, 37, 110
Hazzard, Carolyn 26, 27, 80
Heffner, Elyse 103
Heritage Parade 72
Hewitt, Kelsey 81
History Center of Traverse City 9
Hodge, David 72
Holmer, Signe 23, 80
Hoover, President Herbert 23, 26
Houdek, Amy 81
House of Flavors 43
Howard, Meg 81

I

India 42
Interlochen 48
Interlochen Arts Academy 39
Interlochen Arts Camp 48
Interlochen Center for the Arts 48
International Festival Association 50

J

James Bond 37
James, Henry 54
Japanese attack on Pearl Harbor 29
Jennett, Jeremy 109
John Minnema Memorial Trophy 54
Johnson, George M. 20
Johnson, Richard 59
Junior Royale Parade 71

K

Kaberle, Kelli 66, 81
Kalahar, Leo P. 20
Kardes, Mary 39, 80
Kearns, Charlotte 80
Kelly, Lisa 10, 106
Kelly, Sue 9, 111
Kennedy, John F. 38
Kern, Tom 71, 72
Kilwin's 90
Kimmel, Husband E. 29
King, Janet 109
King, John 69
Kingsley 57
Kiwanis Club 20, 71
Kogelman, Miranda 81
Kolt, Leif 94
Krahnke, Gail 80
Krishna Consciousness 60
Kroupa, Ethel 44
Kula, Kelly 81

L

LaCross, Maria 81
LaFranier, Josephine 43
Lahym, Kay 80
Lake Bluff Stables 44
Lansing 39
Laura the Elephant 65
LaVene, Fred 41
Leelanau County Cherry Home Canning Company 15
LeFranier, Josephine 27, 80
Leno, Jay 66
Library of Congress 11
Light and Power Plant 65
Lindsey, George 48
Lindsey, Trudy Ann 80
Ludington Daily News 9, 26, 27, 49, 52, 63, 69, 71
Lyon, Eliene 28, 80

M

Mackey, Jen 95
Mackinac Bridge Authority 29
Magee, Kevin 67
Manistee 23
Manney, Ardis 80
Mardi Gras 32, 44
Maryland 51
Maud Miller Hoffmaster Art Gallery 43
Maurer, Anne 80
Mavety, Rebecca, "Miss Mancelona" 43
Maxwell, Paula Ann 80
Mayberry RFD 48
McIntyre, Reba 66
McKay, Mitzie 80
McManus, Frank 39
McManus, George 51, 61
Meloche, Evenl 80
Menzel, Tom 72
Mercola, Dr. Joseph 92
Meyer Jewelry 42
Michels, Christie 80
Michels, Christine 29
Michels, Rodolfo 29
Michigan 12, 13, 14, 23, 24, 26, 29, 32, 33, 39, 40, 41, 48, 51, 54, 60, 61, 62, 63, 68, 69, 74, 84, 95, 106
Michigan State Police 69
Michigan State University 92
Michigan Transit Company 20
Micro Brew and Music Festival 77
midway 29
Midwest 49
Millard, Mitchell 104

INDEX

Milliken, Governor 52
Milliken, James T. 20
Milliken, Mrs. Wm. G. 51
Milwaukee Journal 62
Miss Curwood Festival 70
Miss Elk Rapids 83
Mona Lisa 37
Moonies 59, 60
Moon, Sun Myung 59
Morgan, B.J. 14, 15
Morgan, Don 17
Moss, Danielle 81
Mount Pleasant 43
Mr. Cherry 74
Muller Baking Company 39
mummers 39, 41
Munson Medical Center 54
Murray, Dorinda 80

N

National Broadcasting Company 26
National Cherry Festival 7, 8, 9, 11, 12, 17, 21, 23, 24, 26, 27, 28, 29, 30, 32, 33, 37, 38, 39, 40, 41, 42, 43, 44, 46, 47, 48, 49, 50, 51, 52, 54, 55, 59, 60, 61, 62, 63, 66, 67, 68, 70, 72, 73, 74, 76, 77, 78, 79, 81, 89, 92, 94, 97, 100, 107, 108, 110, 111, 112, 115, 116, 125
National Cherry Festival queen 8, 9, 11, 20, 23, 24, 26, 27, 28, 29, 32, 33, 39, 41, 42, 43, 44, 47, 48, 50, 51, 53, 59, 60, 61, 65, 66, 69, 70, 71, 74, 79, 80, 81, 82, 83, 84, 85, 86, 87, 110
National Cherry Industry Administrative Board 69
National Democratic Convention in Chicago 29
National Music Camp 48
National Observatory 36
Neihardt, Alison 107
Newman, Dorothy 59

Newton, John H. 28
New York City 23
Nicula, Jameson 104
Nicula, Wesley 103
Nolan, Helen 53
Nolan, Mary Jane 80
Northern Michigan 8, 26
Northern Natural Cider House 9, 95
Northwestern Michigan College 69
Noye, Bea 51
Nugent, Jim 63, 68

O

Observer 51
Oldham, Morella 26, 80
Old Mission Peninsula 14, 21
Oleson 78
Olney, Susan Beth 80
Open Space 63, 65, 100
Osborne, Chase 24
Owosso Argus Press 33, 41

P

Pacific Fleet 29
Panchame, Nick 92
Paramount Coffee 89
Park Place 39, 44
Park Place Dome 44
Park Place Hotel 44, 89
Park Place Motor Inn 39
Pearce, David 42
Pearl Harbor 28, 29
Pearson, Marion 41
Pepera, Genevieve 80
Petertyl, Sandra 30
Petertyl, Willard 30
Phillips, Nancy 80
Piggot, Lori 95
Pinestead 43
Pleva, Cindy 80
Plucinski, Kelly 9, 80, 81, 84
Polus, Marlene 80
Powell, Cheryl 80
Pratt, Carl 53

Index

Pratt, Fred H. 20
Prusick, Ashley 81

Q

Quincy, Illinois 69

R

Raansaane 44
Raitt, Bonnie 66
Rajah 42
Rajah's Lost Crown 41
Record Eagle 20, 41, 47, 54, 71, 73, 78
Red Cherry Institute 47
Red Star Squadron 69
Red Wings 95
Reitz, Michele 80
Reynolds-Jonkhoff Funeral Home 13
Rhem, Mallory 102
Rider, Lois Jean 80
Right Brain Brewery 9, 92, 94, 95
Robson, Earl 41
Rodenroth, Iali 103
Rodriguez, Don 68
Rokos Drug Store 39
Rolsen, Rebecca Jean 80
Romney, George 39, 44
Roosevelt, Eleanor 26
Rose Bowl 86
Rosenbaum, Meyer 42
Ross, Patricia 110
Rotary Charity 67
Rotary Club 20, 71

S

Saito, Hiroshi 28
Sales, Soupy 51
San Antonio 50
San Antonio Express 50
Sanders, "Colonel" 51
Sanford, Elaine 80
Sayler, Angela 81
Sayler, Sonya 81
Schaller, Don 68

Schlimme, Jessica 9
Schlitz Beer 51
Schmidt, Geri 80
Schneider, Maggie 70, 81
Schroeder, Kaley 81
Schroeder, Kaley Lynn 69
Scott, Willard 60, 67
Seabees 43
7 Monks 51
Shapkaroff, Kate 107
Sherwood, C.G. 17
Shoemaker, Bob 50
Siciliano, Peg 9
Smith, Jay P. 20, 21
Smith, Susan 80
South Vietnam 47
Springsteen, Russell 92
Stallman, Spencer 102
Starr, Ringo 65
Steele, Lori Hall 115
St. Ignace 29
St. Petersburg, Florida 50
Students for Life 71
Sullivan, Erin 81
Sundown Motel 39
Super Cherry 74, 76
Sutherland, Paul 90
Sweet and Snappy Cherry Drinks 115

T

Tama (cruiser) 28
Tamarkin, Louis 42
Taylor, Chloe 101
Thirlby Field 33, 54
Thunderbirds 57
Tirck, Jacob Alin 102
Titus, Harold 20
Tkach, Trevor 7, 8, 9, 73
Toledo Blade 66, 68
Tompkins, Murrie 43, 80
Tornberg, Melissa 80
Tournament of Roses 32
Toxic Cherries 96
Trapp, Mary Lonn 80

Traverse City 7, 8, 9, 11, 12, 13, 14, 15, 17, 20, 21, 23, 26, 27, 28, 30, 32, 33, 39, 41, 43, 47, 48, 50, 51, 52, 53, 54, 57, 58, 60, 61, 62, 66, 67, 68, 69, 72, 73, 76, 77, 78, 89, 90, 94, 95, 96, 97, 105, 106, 108, 110, 111, 112, 113, 115, 116, 125
Traverse City Boom Boom Club 73
Traverse City Centennial 30
Traverse City Cherry Bombs 96
Traverse City Film Festival 77, 116
Traverse City Roller Derby (TCRD) 9, 95, 97, 104, 112
Traverse City Senior Center 9
Traverse City Senior High School 61
Traverse City Wolves 95
Treasure Chest collection 42

U

Umulis, Megan 81
Union Street 51
United States Air Force 57
U.S. Department of Agriculture 63
USO China Beach 48
USS *Astoria* 28

V

Vandenberg, Arthur 26, 29
Vanderbush, Brooks 125
VanderSteen, Joy 80
Vang, Mai Ia 105
Veliquette, Sara 80
Verno, Vonnie 80
Vietnam 46, 47, 48

W

Waddell Buick garage 35
Wakefield, Lucille and Lawrence 9
Wake Island 29
Walker, Ivy 100
Walker, Kimmy 23
Walkmeyer, Dorothy L. 48, 50

Wallace, George C. 37
Wamsley, Marcia 80
Washington, D.C. 23, 26
Washington, George 59
Weaver, Maxine 80
Weeks, Don 53
Wertman, George 86
Williamsburg 39
Wills, Christina 80
Wilson, Laura 9
World News This Morning 67
World War II 29

Y

Yarnell, Trudy 52, 80
York, Anna May 80

Z

Zietes 44
Zinth, Kristopher 108
ZZ Top 65

ABOUT THE AUTHOR

Brooks Vanderbush has lived and worked in the Grand Traverse region for most of his life. During the day, he is a fearless marketer, spreading the message of the arts throughout the world.

When he's not wearing a marketer's hat, he is completely engulfed in the world of writing. He has been a staff writer, editor and freelance journalist in the Grand Traverse region for over a decade now, covering everything from presidential elections to hometown garage sales. He knows and loves this region and all that it has to offer.

His writing has taken him from Traverse City to years of living in Guatemala and many points between. He currently lives in Traverse City with his wife and three children, Jameson, Wesley and Archer.

He *will* be at the National Cherry Festival. Every year. Because he loves it.

Visit us at
www.historypress.net

This title is also available as an e-book